MW01062632

The 7 Rings of Marriage is a uni< riage. Marriages either grow or book will definitely help you have a growing marriage. I highly recommend it to couples of all ages.

—**Gary D. Chapman**, author of *The Five Love Languages*

I've been following Jackie's story for a while now. Humble, insightful, and revealing, Jackie is more than an inspiration. He's like a marriage GPS. His "7 Rings" model can show you exactly where your relationship is and where it's going. And it's grounded in the kind of personal experience that proves the program.

—**Michael Hyatt**, *New York Times* best-selling author and blogger, MichaelHyatt.com

I have been absolutely amazed to watch the trajectory of Jackie Bledsoe's influence. He is quickly becoming the thought leader in matters of family and fatherhood. He is already an influence in my life. This book captures perfectly the mind and heart of Jackie. I predict it will become a classic in the ministry of marriage and parenting.

—**Thom S. Rainer**, president and CEO, LifeWay Christian Resources

Jackie Bledsoe was able to write this book only because he's living it! I have been honored to be a part of Jackie's life over the past few years, and I have seen him experience these various Rings of marriage that every couple encounters at some point. Pay close attention to what you read, then put it into practice. The result will be a better, more loving marriage that brings you years of pleasure.

—**Kevin B. Bullard**, president, Marriage Works!, www.marriageworks.us

The 7 Rings of Marriage delivers a powerful message: husbands and wives can love one another as God intended, even during the tough times. Jackie gives specific guidelines to help us address the challenges in marriage that are sure to come, and shines a light on the safest path to progress.

—**Mark and Susan Merrill**, founders of Family First,
All Pro Dad, and iMOM

Every couple starts marriage with a lot of hope. We hope the longer we are married, the better our marriage will be. But for many couples that isn't the case . . . Longer married doesn't always equate to a better marriage. What I love about *The 7 Rings of Marriage* is the infusion of hope Jackie gives each of us in our marriage relationship. No matter where you are in your marriage you will find practical and insightful truths that move you closer to God and closer to the person you love most. Don't just buy this book . . . read it, absorb it and apply it.

—**Justin Davis**, author of *Beyond Ordinary: When a Good
Marriage Just Isn't Good Enough*

The 7 Rings of Marriage is a refreshing resource that has the power to help marriages in a really practical way. Jackie's approach to helping married couples understand the state of their marriage and how they can move forward in their relationship is clearly explained as he describes each of the 7 Rings. This book is timely. Our hope is that husbands and wives invest into their marriage by reading this book together, challenging themselves to continue on strong in their marriage.

—**Aaron and Jennifer Smith**, founders of
HusbandRevolution.com and Unveiledwife.com

Jackie Bledsoe is an extraordinary leader. In a time where many couples only want to share the "front stage" of their marriage with others, Jackie has the courage to take you behind the scenes and show you the "back stage." He is transparent about the failures and successes of his own marriage and teaches you how tough times can serve as lessons learned if you allow them to. From leading his own family well to teaching you how to lead and love yours, this book will transform your marriage. Transparent, authentic and honest, his 7 Rings Model will not only give you hope for the future, but will show you how to put that hope in action.

—**Jevonnah "Lady J" Ellison,** leading purpose strategist and founder of Maximum Potential Academy

The 7 Rings of Marriage is a true gift to couples. Jackie's practical and relatable style makes it easy to enjoy the 7 Rings principles and, more importantly, put them into practice to make a real difference in everyday married life. Living an awesome marriage isn't easy, but it's absolutely worth it—and this book provides a road map to make it happen.

—**Dustin Riechmann,** author of *15 Minute Marriage Makeover* and founder of EngagedMarriage.com

Setting the right expectations for marriage is essential for couples that want to go the distance, but it seems today marriage is a thick fog that leaves so many confused and hopeless. Consider this a hand to lead you out. Jackie holds nothing back in sharing his struggles and failures as a way to provide you hope that you can have your happily ever after!

—**Casey and Meygan Caston,** cofounders of Marriage365.com

Jackie's and Stephana's passion for all of us to have the best possible marriage no matter our present circumstances permeates every page of this book! Jackie becomes our brother sharing his failures and successes. He and Stephana draw you in with their incredible transparency, humor, time-tested practical marriage tips, and provide marriage evaluation tools. With more than thirty years in marriage ministry, *The 7 Rings of Marriage* is a resource I'll use with all my clients!

—**Clarence Shuler,** president and CEO, BLR: Building Lasting Relationships

The 7 Rings of Marriage is a must read for all couples, from new-lyweds to those couples who have been together for decades. Each Ring will deepen your understanding of marriage and you will be able to equip yourself to have the marriage you desire. You will see how each Ring is connected to one another giving you the vision for an extraordinary marriage . . . a marriage where you are fully present, intentional, and continually growing together. Jackie's insights, stories and passion will have you wanting more.

—**Tony and Alisa DiLorenzo,** ONE Extraordinary Marriage, cohosts of the #1 Marriage Podcast on iTunes

A few years ago, my wife and I bought a *Fireproof* DVD for every couple we know as Christmas gifts. Now I know what I'll be giving for Christmas this year! *The 7 Rings of Marriage* is powerful. Touching. Honest. And most important, I can put this information into practice TODAY.

—**Donnie Bryant,** copywriter, founder of Donnie-Bryant.com

The 7 Rings of Marriage is one of the most amazing tools to grow a healthy marriage out there!

—**Eric Dingler,** campus pastor, NewPointe Community Church

What I love most about this book is the author lives its message. I've been following Jackie's story for years now and have seen him love his wife and kids up close and personal. If you want to learn how to do marriage and family right from someone who walks the walk, read this book.

—**Jeff Goins,** best-selling author of *The Art of Work*

The **7** *Rings of*

MARRIAGE

The **7** *Rings of*

MARRIAGE

Your Model for
a Lasting and Fulfilling
Marriage

JACKIE BLEDSOE

Nashville, Tennessee

To my wife, Stephana . . .

I thank God for you. Throughout this process, through the emotional ups and downs, and through some occasional "tantrums," you have been there to listen, to share, and to help me grind it out. There is absolutely no way I could have done this without you. Nor is there any way I could do, or ever want to do, life without you. So, I say, "thank you," and "I love you."

Contents

Introduction

Marriage is not what it used to be.
Marriage is under attack.
Marriage is what you make of it.
Marriage is "the legally formalized union . . ."
Marriage has so many descriptions, labels, and definitions. Couples today are confused. They don't truly know what marriage is. They don't see enough models for lasting and fulfilling marriages. Due to this they are lacking hope in their marriages and uncertain if they will make it.

Maybe you are one of those couples. You have questions but not enough answers. You want more in marriage but don't know how to get more. You may not believe more is even possible in your marriage.

My wife and I had the same questions and concerns early in our marriage. We had our first child before we had even considered marriage, then tied the knot ten months later. We quickly felt like our marriage was under attack or, better yet, that we both were under attack from one another.

I guess we should have expected some tough times. After all our marriage started with a honeymoon that was something we barely speak of to this day. Following are some of the "highlights" from our honeymoon. Upon arrival to our destination, we were almost too afraid to get out of the car. My wife decided to sleep on the couch, refusing to sleep in the bed. The most memorable meal (and not a good memory) we had on our honeymoon was some rubbery fried chicken that the bugs swarming around us probably enjoyed more than we did. It was by all accounts not the ideal way to start a marriage.

In addition to our unforgettable honeymoon, we've experienced many more bumps and bruises. We've shared the hurt from failed marriages of family and close friends. We know from our own experience what real marriage struggle looks and feels like. But we also know what the experiences of lasting and fulfilling marriages are like. Our marriage has been molded through the lessons our own bumps and bruises have taught us, as well as a watchful eye on other successful marriages. And we are the benefactors of marriage mentors who have poured their hearts, insights, and lives into our relationship.

In this book I will not only share with you "what marriage is," but I will share our marriage-transforming experiences to open your eyes to the type of marriage that is possible for you. You'll see the big picture as well as the fine details of the marriage masterpiece. All of which will help you experience more in your marriage.

My wife and I, as well as many of our friends, were caught off guard with what happens in marriage. Had we known what we now know, we could have saved some headaches, some heartaches, and some marriages.

I've written for several years on a wide range of marriage-related topics. And I've studied marriage, my own and others, for even more years. Through this I firmly believe marriage is something that was created to last and to be fulfilling.

That's where the 7 Rings of Marriage came from. The rings came from the experiences and journey of not only our marriage but also from other couples who have experienced a marriage that stands the test of time and fulfills what both husband and wife need in their marriage.

I will warn you though, these experiences don't come without risk, and it's not "all good" all of the time. Some stories I will share in this book I've never mentioned publicly, or at least not in detail, because of embarrassment and the feeling that I've failed as a husband and the leader of my family.

By sharing this with you, I hope you gain a deeper appreciation of what marriage is and get a clear picture of what may lie ahead in your marriage. Then I hope you diligently go about making your marriage everything you and your spouse hoped for and more.

Chapter One

When Your Dream Becomes a Nightmare

"Marriage isn't for you."
—Seth Adam Smith's dad

T hink back to your wedding day, better yet the day you proposed to your wife, or your husband proposed to you. Do you remember how you felt—whether you were excited, nervous, or even scared? You were probably thinking about the wonderful life you were about to share together.

Marriage Is Risky Business

Few of you were thinking about the risk of marriage versus the reward. In reality, marriage is a huge risk today. Some studies report that as many as half of all marriages end in divorce. That doesn't even include married couples that don't divorce but live together *unhappily* ever after, or just live apart. Why would you risk that?

What else do we commit so much to that has such a high probability of failure? There must be a pretty high reward to risk that much. Think about it this way: Would you deposit your hard-earned money in the bank if, when the time came to pay your bills, you had only a 50 percent chance that money would be there? The bank would have to promise you a pretty hefty reward for that risk. Or would you show up to work each week, at least five days per week, and spend eight to ten hours per day working, if when payday came around, you had a 50-50 chance your check was going to be cut? I'm guessing you're shaking your head no right now.

So, when it comes to marriage, knowing the risks, why do it? Why even get married? This seems to be the thought on many couples' minds as fewer couples are getting married today than ever before. Part of the reason for the decline is they don't know why you should get married. They only see the why-you-shouldn't-get-married part of it. And that comes with a 50-50 shot at divorce.

What Are Your Reasons for Getting Married?

Those that do get married can inadvertently increase their chances of divorce. Their reasons for getting married make it more risky and more likely to fail. It's kind of like me going into an ice cream store looking to get my desire fulfilled for a soft taco, burrito, or nachos. (Three of my favorites!) No matter how much I like them, or how good it looks when I imagine eating them, or how excited I am about filling that void in my stomach and pleasing my taste buds, I'm going to fail at fulfilling those desires. I can hope or even try to force the person behind the counter to make me a taco, but waffle cones aren't going to work out too well in lieu of taco shells. And I doubt they have lettuce, salsa, cheese, beans, or guacamole in the back. It just doesn't make sense for me to try to get something from a place that has other purposes when it comes to meeting my need for food.

Learning what marriage is can help lower the risk of wanting tacos or burritos when rocky road and vanilla ice cream are really what I should be looking to get out of the store.

When you determine the what, the who, and the value in marriage, you can have a better success rate. If you don't get these things straight, then what was intended to last forever may end way sooner than that. What was intended to be a means for two people to enjoy fulfillment becomes something that takes more than it gives. The fairy-tale dreams become nightmares for many people. And it's getting such a bad name that people who have never experienced it are having nightmares in advance; thus they are deciding to not even go that route. They're saying forget tacos and ice cream! Neither are going to agree with my stomach! Crazy analogy I know, but it works. Because if you wanted tacos and someone is trying to get ice cream down your throat, or vice versa, you aren't going to be pleased!

So, how do you prevent your dreams of an amazing, long-lasting, and truly fulfilling marriage from becoming nightmares of dissatisfaction, frustration, wasted years, and broken hearts? First, you need to know the purpose of marriage.

Assembly Instructions

I've only recently discovered the power of Amazon and ordering online. I know I'm late, way late to the party, but I'm now on board. Part of my objection to ordering things online was due to the fact I couldn't touch, feel, or test it out. My love language is physical touch, and apparently my shopping language is too. Plus the first few items I ordered online, several years ago, I had to return. In fairness to Amazon, I used another online store to purchase these items. I order stuff all the time now. And although I can't touch and feel it before ordering it, I can check out the reviews, read about the manufacturer, and in some cases I can even pull up instruction manuals and find out what all is in the box. I love that!

Once my package comes, I open it up; and if it's something that needs assembling, I pull out the assembly instructions, determine what pieces are included, and note how each piece will be used. That's the important part when trying to put stuff together. I need to know what all this stuff is for. What purpose does it serve, and what intended outcome am I supposed to get?

Marriage is the same way. In order to find out what marriage is for, what's the purpose, and what's the intended outcome, we need some help. In the case of my Amazon shipments, that help comes from the manufacturer, who was wise enough to provide me with a set of instructions to tell me what these various parts are for and the intended outcome for them. In the case of marriage, I go to the Manufacturer in much the same way. Who created marriage and for what purpose?

The Bible tells me that God created marriage, and He even gave the first married couple some great info on what marriage is for. That's where we all need to begin, on the Manufacturer's floor.

Just about everyone who has heard or read anything about the Bible knows the story of Adam and Eve. During this story of creation and the beginning of humankind, God put Adam to sleep, took out his rib, closed him up, and made that rib into a woman intended to be Adam's wife. Just like that manufacturer who made the first prototype of the items I buy off Amazon, God knew those of us who weren't there on the Manufacturer's floor would someday want this "product" called marriage and would need to know what He created it for. These instructions start in Genesis 1 and 2.

Taking a look at this passage will get you on the right path and help you limit the risk of having dreams become nightmares. Let's examine the reasons God created marriage through His "assembly instructions."

A Complement

Adam was a hard worker, and he had the wisdom and skills to take care of the entire garden and name all the creatures God made. But none of those animals complemented him, engaged his mind, or made him better (Gen. 2:20). So God created a complement. Not someone to serve him or to help fulfill his agenda, but a complement to bring the best out of him. When I think about my wife, I see firsthand how He did this in our marriage. I talk fast; she talks slowly. I enjoy planning—I mean like *really* enjoy planning, which results in me taking forever before actually doing anything. She doesn't need or want to plan—I mean like never, ever, ever wants to plan. I am naive when it comes to people's intentions while she has great discernment. The list goes on and on. I had plenty of friends before marriage, both male and female, and a few girlfriends; but none of them ever complemented me like my wife does. Adam had many beings around him, but none of them ever complemented him like Eve. In a later chapter I'll share stories of how God used my wife to improve me and me to improve her.

Intimacy

Prior to their sin, Adam and Eve were naked and felt no shame (Gen. 2:25). Being naked means being vulnerable, or unguarded. It's being exposed. In marriage, both husband and wife can be vulnerable, yet without shame. Just like Adam and Eve, we sin. Sometimes our sin can be embarrassing. (It should be embarrassing all the time, right?) Sometimes we have fears, doubts, and emotional insecurities. With the friendship of our spouse, we can share those things, or become unguarded and exposed without shame. There aren't many people, if any, with whom you can share that same level of vulnerability. In marriage, we've been given a person we can do things with and share things with that we don't do or share with anyone else. Unfortunately many couples today are trying to do those things without the commitment or umbrella of marriage. But that's another story, one I'll share later about how choices like that led to some challenges that plagued our relationship.

Produce with Pleasure

The instructions given to the first male and female were to produce. "Be fruitful, multiply, fill the earth" (Gen. 1:28). And the beauty of it all is He blessed us with a gift of pleasure in it. "Let your fountain be blessed, and take pleasure in the wife of your youth"

(Prov. 5:18). The Bible repeatedly instructs us to be fruitful and multiply (see also Gen. 9:1 and 9:7). This is a continuation of the intimacy discussed earlier. When a married couple becomes one physically, they are coming to know each other in a deeper, more intimate way. And from this comes one of the most amazing miracles any of us has ever seen or experienced—the miracle of birth and children. Depending on who is reading this, this may be where the pleasure part ends. (Childbirth is painful and raising kids can be, too.) Our children can definitely impact the pleasure part of the intimate relationship with our spouse. Nonetheless, having children and producing something together is one of the great reasons and purposes for marriage.

Stewardship

God has given us everything on this earth to use and enjoy. He didn't spare anything with His amazing creation. In our mates He's given us someone to bring out the best in us. He's given us someone we can share things with that we don't share with anybody else. And He's blessed us in marriage so we can produce and fill the earth with pleasure. Our task is to care for and manage what He's given us. His command was for us to subdue the earth and rule over it (Gen. 1:28). Similar to the way Adam and Eve managed the garden, how Adam gave the animals their names, and both of them cared for it all. Adam and Eve's marriage wasn't just for them. Although they experienced plenty of enjoyment and pleasure within marriage, the purpose of their marriage was bigger. They had a responsibility together to carry out, to steward, and to manage an amazing part of God's magnificent plan.

In the purpose for marriage, God has given us something to meet our needs. He's given us a way to connect mentally, emotionally, and physically to each other and ultimately a way for us to have a better understanding and deeper connection to Him spiritually.

When you understand these reasons for marriage, you can make sure you aren't doing the equivalent of ordering tacos at an ice cream parlor. You can prevent your marriage dreams from becoming marriage nightmares and actually experience a long-lasting and truly fulfilling marriage.

More Risky Not to Get Married

When I began my final college semester, my posteducation plans, or plan for my life, consisted of "move to LA to live with my sister (from my little old school in Florence, South Carolina)." First, it was a shock to me, and everybody else, that I was going to graduate on time. Let's just say I was not the best student, and my vision was limited. Basically, the upcoming weekend was about as far as my planning skills would take me at the time, in stark contrast to the way I approach my future now.

Fast-forward to a few months before I graduated, and my "plans" took a drastic hit. My sister accepted a job close to home in Indianapolis. Wow! The reality of my actually being able to graduate in four years had just set in, and no sooner than that my life plan was messed up by my sister's new job. So I adjusted and made new plans. My new plan was to find a job, any job, in Indianapolis, where my sister lived, or Dayton, Ohio, where my brother lived. Our hometown of Richmond, Indiana, was just about the halfway point between the two. Well, a job in Indianapolis set those plans in motion.

I moved to Indy, started working in the insurance field, and was on my way. I continued on that path until a friend introduced me to a book. The book was called *Rich Dad Poor Dad* by Robert Kiyosaki. That was one of two books that changed my plans and impacted the course of my life more than any other books, other than the Bible, at that time. It forced me to look at things differently and as Kiyosaki would put it to "mind my business."[1]

Minding my business basically meant while I was doing my best working whatever job I had at the time, I also needed to mind my own personal finances and my sources of income—in other words, my "business." This thinking was that as long as I was minding other people's business, my employer and the undisciplined way in which I spent my money, then I was subject to their choices and other external factors. To Kiyosaki that was risky business. I soon learned why he felt that way firsthand when I lost my job for the first time. The insurance company I was working for was downsizing, but I was able to find a new job at a different company shortly before many cuts happened in my department. Ironically, I lost the new job about a year and a half later. That would be the first of two times I lost a job.

The negative impact it had on my family and our lifestyle left me bitter, to a degree, toward corporate America and working for someone else. After the first job loss my entrepreneur endeavors were launched. And since then, as hard as it has been to be an entrepreneur—from no guaranteed checks, to high health insurance costs, to no days off, to trying to balance work and family when it all happens in the same place—it has never seemed that risky to me. Many people couldn't believe how I could have such a high-risk tolerance when it came to the way I provided for my family. I viewed it just the opposite. Working a regular job or working for someone else was riskier than being an entrepreneur.

And I say the same about marriage. Yes, there is a risk that you may get married and your marriage doesn't make it. As I shared earlier, some studies say that risk is as high as 50–50. But that also means there is a 50 percent chance your marriage will make it. The benefits of getting married and staying married far outweigh the risk of getting married and potentially getting divorced, as well as the risk of not getting married at all.

Had I not ventured out on my own in pursuit of my entrepreneurial dreams, then you wouldn't be reading this book right now. The risk I took gave me the freedom to pursue my passion. The risk

I took gave me the freedom to spend as much, or as little, time with my family as I desired. The risk I took allowed me to trust in the greatest "security blanket" there has ever been, God's Word.

My marriage has been the same. The marriage risk I took gave me the freedom to love in a way I had never done before when I committed to one person instead of only giving part of me to many people. The marriage risk I took gave me the courage to stand for something that many people in the world today are tearing down and trying to redefine. The marriage risk I took forced me to know, depend on, and serve my wife, my family, and my God in an amazing way.

I'll take those odds any day! If those reasons aren't practical enough for you, the Center for Marriage and Families shares the following info from some research they've done, highlighting some of the major benefits of marriage.

1. Children are more likely to enjoy family stability when they are born into a married family.
2. Married couples build more wealth on average than singles or cohabiting couples.
3. Marriage is associated with better health and lower rates of injury, illness, and disability for both men and women.
4. Children whose parents divorce have higher rates of psychological distress and mental illness.
5. Marriage appears to reduce the risk that adults will be either perpetrators or victims of crime.[2]

Being married, and staying married, has a tremendous impact on many areas of our lives including our families, our money, our health, our mental and emotional well-being, and our safety.

I hope this gives you a mind-set shift when it comes to marriage and its risk. If you are single and considering marriage, hopefully it encourages you and leads you to consider committing to something that can be lasting and fulfilling. If you've already made that commitment but aren't sure if it will last, or if it will ever be fulfilling, hopefully this encourages you and confirms that you took a good risk.

Marriage Isn't for You

So now you have a better idea of the purpose of marriage. There are some great and wonderful things within marriage, but is marriage for everybody? More important, is marriage for you?

Let me say this. . . . *Marriage isn't for you.*

If you thought marriage is for you up to this point, then I'm sorry to have misled you. Or maybe I just didn't share enough to enable you to have the full breadth of marriage. If it makes you feel any better, marriage isn't for me either.

Do you wonder how can I say that? I mean, I know me, I know my wife, and I know our marriage. However, I don't know you, your relationship, or anything about your spouse. But it still applies, and this is what makes that simple statement so profound. I've learned that simplicity usually is what makes for good advice, albeit shocking sometimes.

Let me explain. But first let me say this. I learned this from somebody else. I don't know the gentleman's name, so I'm going to call him Seth Adam Smith's dad. Seth Adam Smith is a blogger who wrote a blog post that could make the argument for being the most popular marriage advice ever given, at least on the Internet. In Seth's blog post he shared the biggest marriage lesson he received from his father. It was that simple statement, "Marriage isn't for you." Let's unpack the depth in this simple statement.

What I believe he is saying is marriage is 100 percent unselfish. At least it's supposed to be. It isn't for you, your satisfaction, or your joy. It is about the person you are marrying and everybody else that is connected to that union, like your children. Marriage is 100 percent unselfish. At no point in time is it 100 percent for you.

Here is a quote from Seth's dad that Seth shared on his website:

Seth, you're being totally selfish. So I'm going to make this really simple: marriage isn't for you. You don't marry to make yourself happy, you marry to make someone else happy. More than that, your marriage isn't for yourself, you're marrying for a family. Not just for the in-laws and all of that nonsense, but for your future children. Who do you want to help you raise them? Who do you want to influence them? **Marriage isn't for you.** It's not about you. Marriage is about the person you married.[3]

How does that change your perspective on marriage, and how you've been doing things in your marriage? It sure changed my perspective. While I knew early in our marriage that I was selfish, this reminded me and exposed the fact that I hadn't changed much. I still wanted things to be about me, not about her, or you, or anybody else. Most marriages fail because each person thinks marriage is for them, not the person they married. Realizing marriage isn't for you, and following up with action that backs this up, requires making the choice to be selfless over and over again. So, remember, marriage isn't for you. Not today, not tomorrow, not next week, not never. (Sometimes it takes a double negative to drive a point home.) Hopefully by now you have a better idea of what marriage is for and more important, whom it's for, which is not you.

I did a Google search for "marriage quotes." The search returned a staggering amount of results, over 500 million. That is a lot of quotes about marriage. It must be pretty important, pretty valuable, or at least frequently talked about. After clicking on a few of them, I found it was indeed popular, but I'm sad to say not necessarily valued by everyone. Many of the quotes were negative or in jest. Marriage and marriage experiences are the butt of many online jokes. I do have a sense of humor and found some of them funny. But overall

I came away thinking that marriage has little to no value today. Marriage is a laughing matter to many people. Perhaps this is why the divorce rates are where they are, because it's not taken seriously.

"A good marriage would be between a blind wife and a deaf husband."

"One should always be in love. That is the reason one should never marry."

"Politics doesn't make strange bedfellows—marriage does."

Those are just a few of the specific quotes I found in my Google search. It had me thinking back to when I decided to get married. I had one friend who was married at the time. One. I had zero friends who wanted to get married. Zero.

And that isn't just the male perspective, which you may expect among men below the age of twenty-five. My wife didn't have any friends who were married either. But we both had friends who were doing things married people do together, without the commitment. That included us. It confirms what those Google searches revealed. Marriage isn't taken as seriously as it should be. Marriage isn't valued like it was years ago when more couples seemed to get married and stay married.

In many relationships today unmarried people have children. They purchase houses and cars together. They become beneficiaries on insurance policies. These are the same things my wife and I have done and experienced as a married couple.

If you can do all the things a married couple does, what difference does it make if you wear a wedding ring, state some vows, or sign some papers? It seems it doesn't really add any additional value. But if marriage is sacred, there has to be more to it than living together, sleeping together, and having debt together. Especially having debt together.

Placing a High Value on Marriage

The Bible teaches us to leave and cleave. We are even to "leave" the most important relationship we've ever had—the relationship with our parents. That means this thing called marriage is pretty serious; it has a lot of value. So, how do we make our marriages more valuable than any other relationship we have? How can we make it special or sacred? How can we give value to our marriage?

I believe this is one major step on your way to a lasting and fulfilling marriage. Marriage has to have tremendous value. Like the ring your grandmother gave you. Or the Little League trophy you just can't seem to get rid of. Or the little people running around your house that call you Mom or Dad.

Once we do this, once we begin to take marriage seriously and place a higher value on it, we can reduce the risk of divorce and increase the probability that our marriages will last. As a result I believe our perspectives on marriage will change, and maybe we'll see fewer jokes about marriage and instead see more moving and encouraging quotes about marriage and more truth when we search Google. While it's not an overnight change, you can start right now by embracing a few things and taking action accordingly. Below are some things that will help you and your spouse place a high value on your marriage and ultimately make it last. Consider this your first step toward a better marriage.

1. *Friendship.* Can you truly spend your life with someone you are not friends with? Friendship in marriage is crucial. A good friendship is developed through spending time together, communicating, having disagreements, and being selfless. Truly good friends will value marriage. We will discuss much more on being friends with your spouse in later chapters.

2. *Commitment.* A major difference in marriage and a dating relationship is commitment. "Breaking up" or "not seeing

each other anymore" was never part of the design in marriage. Committing to the marriage and committing to your spouse will give more value to that relationship than any other relationship.

3. *Delayed Gratification.* We live in a "right now" society. We want, and many times get, what we desire instantly. Not in marriage. Good marriages are built over time. Love and respect are grown over time. Realizing the investment in your marriage today is going to produce better days in the future will add value to your marriage.

4. *Intimacy.* A mentor of mine defined *intimacy* as "sharing something with a person that you don't share with anyone else." So to be truly intimate in your marriage, some things need to be reserved only for your spouse. Saying and doing things reserved for this one person will add value to your marriage.

5. *Foundation.* Any structure without a solid foundation will likely fall. A marriage must have a solid foundation. Your marriage foundation is what you believe about marriage in general and your marriage specifically. That foundation must be the same for both you and your spouse. The marriage foundation my wife and I stand on is found in the Bible. Without it, our marriage would have fallen long ago. With it, value is added to our marriage, and it is truly precious to us.

Marriage has value, but you have to see it. Reading the statistics, listening to those who devalue or disrespect marriage, or even doing "marriage stuff" without getting married can cause us to place little value on it. Whether you are single or married, I encourage you to place a high value on marriage. After all, nobody wants anything that lacks value, especially a relationship intended to last a lifetime.

Chapter Two

Begin with the End

"Begin with the end in mind."
–Stephen Covey

E very once in a while you read a book that has a lasting impact on your life. One of those books for me is *The 7 Habits of Highly Effective People* by Stephen Covey. When I read the book over ten years ago, my entire perspective changed. But little did I know what I learned in Mr. Covey's book would change the way I look at my marriage as well.

When I read *The 7 Habits*, it wasn't just about being more productive, or about a planning system for handling daily tasks and to-dos. It was a change in the way I viewed life and looked at my future. The most impactful idea to me was habit number two, "Begin with the end in mind."[1]

For those of you who aren't familiar with the seven habits, specifically habit number two, habit two is based on imagination—the ability to envision in your mind what you cannot see at present with your eyes. In summary, it is seeing what you want before achieving it, then working your way backwards with the knowledge of what it takes to get there.

How many married couples have a realistic view of what to expect in their marriage?

Based on the stats that say you have a 50-50 chance to get divorced or stay married (for Christians and non-Christians), I'd say few couples have a realistic view of what to expect.

Embracing the idea of beginning with the end in mind gave me the freedom to see the "big picture" and anticipate what would happen along the way of my life's journey. The same thing can happen in marriage. In fact, it must happen if you don't want to be a part of the "other 50." You have to begin with the end of your marriage in mind, and I'm not talking about divorce. I'm talking about what you want your marriage to look like years from now. Have you thought that far?

How do you want your marriage to end? Divorce? Death?

Most married couples promise, "until death do us part," in their wedding vows. But how do you get there? How do you become old, gray, still married, *and* still in love?

You get there by beginning with the end of your marriage in mind. With that knowledge, and the steps it takes to get there, your marriage will be much better. Your marriage will be lasting and fulfilling.

After years of marriage, observing other marriages, writing and teaching about marriage, and after many conversations with other married couples, I've noticed most couples go through seven stages on their way to a truly lasting and fulfilling marriage. I call them the *7 Rings of Marriage*.

Your Model for a Lasting and Fulfilling Marriage

Knowing the *7 Rings of Marriage* will help you see the big picture and allow you to begin with the end of your marriage in mind. It will help you navigate through the good, the bad, the highs, the lows, and what happens in marriage.

Whether you've been married several years, are newlyweds, or are just considering getting married, you should become familiar with the *7 Rings of Marriage*. Use them to determine where you are in your marriage, what you should do to keep growing your marriage, and ultimately what you can do to make your marriage last with love.

Before we jump into the *7 Rings*, let's take some time to think about the end of your marriage. First, let's be clear. We aren't talking about prenuptial agreements and who will get the house, car, kids, and the china. That's for the "other 50," which, based on the fact you are reading this book, you don't want to be part of that group.

Let's think about how you want your marriage to look when it ends the way God intends a marriage to end. That is, according to the wedding vows, "until death do us part."

What Will People Say?

Considering your own death can be rough, especially for younger couples, but it will provide you with a great perspective that eliminates many of the less important things we focus on throughout our lives.

Let's imagine the following. You are a "fly on the wall" at your very own funeral. Five people will speak.

The first speaker is your spouse; the second is one, or all of your kids; the third is a friend; the fourth is a coworker or business partner; and the fifth is someone from your church or community organization.

Before going further, take a few minutes to write down your thoughts on what you hope they will say about you and, specifically, about your marriage.

If you did this exercise, you should have uncovered what is most important in your life. You should have a clear understanding of the direction you want your marriage to go. But the question is: What will it require for your marriage to get there?

Lessons from Legos

When I was a kid, I didn't play with Legos much. They just didn't move me like other toys and games did. Today my kids play with them all the time, and I've even enjoyed building Lego masterpieces with them. I don't remember having the awesome models of Legos they have today.

When you buy Legos today, they aren't just a bunch of pieces in a box for you to create something out of thin air. No, they are cartoon characters, packages that depict actual scenes from movies, and even small cities.

And each one comes with a model in the form of a picture that includes the step-by-step instructions to create that specific Lego design. My kids can look at the images on the boxes in the store or online and decide which world, scene, and characters they want to create.

They've seen in their minds the end result they want, and now they can begin taking steps to get there. Sometimes they miss steps or pieces, and it doesn't fit correctly. That's when they call me in to help them. They don't want me to do it for them, but they want my advice, or my counsel, to get them back on track.

After taking action on what I've suggested, they immediately resume creating the Lego design they envisioned. Are you getting the connection?

I never stuck with Legos because I felt I was aimlessly going about it. Every time I started, I eventually quit after the newness and excitement wore off. I quit when it became hard to create something that made me feel good. I wanted to create something to be proud of but didn't know how to do it or even what it should look like.

Around 50 percent of marriages experience this today.

Another 50 percent has a different experience. Their experience is more like my kids' experience with Legos. My kids love Legos and can't get enough of them. They want to experience building bigger and better Lego designs.

The major difference is they have a clear model, steps to create what they want, and people to help along the way.

That's what the 7 Rings of Marriage are for you.

We'll start diving into the 7 *Rings* in the next chapter. As you discover them, think about which ring you're wearing today and visualize where you want to go next.

You Don't Know Nothin'

Those are the words from one of the smartest persons I've ever known, my grandfather. He used to say that to us grandkids when we got to the point of asking too many questions or we tried to teach him something he already knew.

But those words weren't just reserved for the grandkids. He'd tell his grown kids, my dad and his brothers, the same thing when they seemed to think they knew more than he did.

Fast-forward thirty plus years, and I still hear those words to this day. Except now they are coming from my dad. And just as my grandfather did not discriminate on whom those words were directed at, my dad doesn't believe in discrimination either.

Well, they say the apple doesn't fall far from the tree. I'm taking the nondiscrimination of those words even further. I'm saying them to you.

You don't know nothin' . . . about marriage.

We all come into marriage with our own ideas of how marriage should be. Even those of us who've been married for a while have expectations of our marriage—better yet, expectations of our spouses that show how much we really don't know about marriage, and how much we need to forget what we thought we knew about marriage.

I know because I continually learn that what I thought about marriage, my marriage specifically, is way off base sometimes. And that is an ongoing process.

For us to see the end of our marriage in the proper perspective, we have to forget some of the ideals we brought into marriage. We also have to forget some of the ideals and expectations we've developed throughout our marriage. It's time to learn what marriage is really about and create a new, shared perspective.

If my wife and I hadn't done that, you wouldn't be reading this book right now, at least not with me as the author. We can honestly say . . .

We don't know nothin' . . . about marriage.

A Shaky Start

Prior to one month before asking my wife to get married, I never dreamed or imagined I'd get married. I never thought about it or thought about whom I'd marry. I never thought I'd get married. I didn't think it was possible. Of course, I had seen plenty of marriages and, without knowing it, had a certain perception of how marriage should function.

Prior to asking my wife to marry me, she also had little, if any, thoughts of marriage. Unlike most women she didn't desire to be married. It was probably one of the last things on her mind.

So there we were, two people who never considered marriage, getting ready to marry each other. We had no basis, no foundation, and definitely no vision of how our marriage would end.

We were literally living marriage minute by minute and moment by emotion-driven moment. For those who do know something about marriage, you know the shaky ground we were standing on.

And it showed, as the first year of our marriage was really hard. We were heading in the wrong direction and fast. But we didn't really know this. We thought we knew something about marriage. No, I thought I knew something about marriage, and Stephana thought she knew something about marriage. Both were two different things.

Had we kept living our marriage from that perspective and not learned new ideals and formed a new perspective, we would have ended up on the wrong side of the marriage statistics.

I could see a lack of intimacy. I could see infidelity. I could see choosing sides in the midst of in-law issues. I could see divorce if nothing changed.

For as much as we thought we knew about marriage, or maybe I should say for as much as we didn't know about marriage, we did know one thing. We knew this was not working.

Hope

We decided to do something. We decided to find out why it wasn't working and what we could do to fix it. Our pursuit led us to taking a marriage class that was being offered by our church. That class confirmed what we found out that first year of marriage, what my grandfather and father had told me, and what I told you earlier . . .

We didn't know nothin' . . . about marriage.

But it didn't discourage us. It opened up our minds. It showed us why we were having problems. And most important, it gave us hope.

We now had hope that we could have a marriage that would last. We now had hope that we could have a marriage that would be fulfilling. Neither of which seemed possible after our experiences of being married for less than a year.

What we learned and experienced in that class, as well as from the people we met, would change the course of our marriage forever. But the journey didn't end with that class. That led us to seek more marriage enrichment activities and experiences, like marriage retreats, more classes, and reading books.

Over time we began to learn a thing or two about marriage. We began to lose those ideals we had about marriage. We began to get rid of unrealistic expectations we had for ourselves and our marriage. We began to forget everything we thought we knew about marriage.

The end result was our new, shared perspective about marriage. We were beginning to "leave and cleave" and beginning to focus less on "I" and more on "she," "he," and "we." It was becoming evident marriage was not for me or for her.

After that class we committed to being lifelong learners about marriage in general and about our own marriage. We could never read one book and know everything about marriage. (*The 7 Rings of Marriage* hadn't been written yet . . . smile.) So we had to continually learn and grow. We had to go on this journey, with a glimpse of what to expect ahead and some tools to help us stay the course.

As we began to implement what we were learning, our circle of friends began to change. We met some couples in the marriage class that made up part of our new circle of friends who wanted more, were seeking more, and were willing to do more in order to have a lasting and fulfilling marriage.

We couldn't have made it no matter how many classes, courses, or retreats we went on without help. Our small group and new inner circle were there for us. But when things progressed past the point of their help, which it did and honestly sometimes still does, we were not afraid to get more help in the form of marriage counseling.

Our marriage was changing, we were changing, and even before we knew it, people were noticing. Our marriage and our purpose in marriage were growing to be bigger and more important than our just being happy and meeting our individual needs.

All because at some point we decided to forget everything we thought we knew about marriage and did something about it.

I don't know where you are in marriage—whether you are engaged, a newlywed, or a seasoned vet. Or whether you are having a hard time, on the brink of divorce, or living the happily-ever-after dream of marriage. It really doesn't matter. Humbling yourself and forgetting what you thought you knew about marriage in order to learn what marriage is really about and create your better, shared perspective will be one of the greatest things you will do for your marriage.

As you read through this book, you will see in detail what we've experienced on this journey as well as what other couples have experienced.

By the time you're finished, my prayer is your perspective will be changed in a way that brings healing, joy, and a sustaining hope. As you progress through the book, you'll be able to begin with the end in mind. You'll be able to determine where your marriage is today and where your focus needs to be to keep it growing, and you'll be able to walk the walk and experience the experiences of a lasting and fulfilling marriage.

I know marriage works. I also know marriage is not easy. My wife and I have been through a lot in our marriage. A lot of it has been heart-wrenching, it has been confusing, and it has taken us to places we never thought we'd be. I wouldn't have it any other way. Our marriage works.

Having a healthy and functional marriage is possible and worth everything you go through on the way. Through it all we can honestly say marriage works, but it has taken our being intentional. We have invested heavily in our marriage. If we hadn't, we wouldn't be married today.

Invest Sooner Rather than Later

We had no idea what we were in for when we were first married. We had known each other for about eight years, but that might as well have been eight days!

Being married was totally different from being friends, significant others, or even baby mammas and daddies. (We had our first child together prior to getting married.) We were in a commitment, a covenant, and had no idea what it was really about or how to make it work.

The class at our church was the first big investment we made in our marriage. From that point on we began to invest in more ways. We signed up to go on a marriage retreat the following summer. We began reading about marriage and how God designed it. Our minds and hearts were opened, and our marriage was literally saved by the things we learned from all of these resources.

Since that point we have made a practice to continually invest in our marriage, and this investment continues to pay off. Although we've "only" been married fourteen years, technology has made marriage-building materials much more available today than when we were getting started.

Blogs, e-books, audio, and video resources are all available twenty-four hours a day, seven days a week.* I am constantly reading, listening to, and watching things that can help me be a better husband for my wife. You are already taking a step to make an investment into your marriage by reading this book.

This investment has the ability to extend the life of your relationship and make your marriage work. I prayed throughout the process of writing this book, along with many others who joined me in doing so, that this book will be the best investment and the timely answer to prayers for our marriages.

My wife and I have experienced a lot in our fourteen years of marriage. Good, bad, exciting, sad, and everything in between. We've witnessed the marriages of several friends end in divorce. We have friends who knew us "back in the day" who would have never imagined us still together.

It's always been on my mind why and how we made it when so many of our peers didn't. Our circumstances and challenges weren't much different, and many were worse, but we are still here. Kind of like the saying, "You live to fight another day." It has perplexed me at times. Now I believe I've discovered it, and I'm certain if it worked in our marriage it will work in yours. Two words served as the glue

* Visit my website for additional resources.

to keep us together and the inspiration to push us forward. Decide to make these two words a benchmark in your marriage journey as you move forward.

No

While taking that class a few months after getting married, we learned God hates divorce, and it should never be an option in our marriage. And until we ruthlessly eliminated that option of divorce from our marriage, it would always be a possibility. So we said no to divorce once and for all in our marriage. It was never to be considered, joked about, or mentioned in our marriage whatsoever! Ever!

Was that easy? No way, not by any means. There were times we both felt trapped. Trapped with each other in our relationship and trapped in our current circumstances. Many times we questioned our decision to get married in the first place. But we remained true to our agreement and stood on this foundational principle. Sometimes we let emotions, anger, and stupidity get the best of us. But *no* was the word anytime thoughts of divorce tried to creep in.

Taking this stance put our backs against the wall and forced us to make our marriage work. Doing so makes you fight together instead of against your spouse. Our choice was to remain married unhappily or find a way to remain married happily. Divorce was not in the equation.

Yes

More recently we have come to understand that our marriage is being watched. And not just because we post all our business on social media. But other people, beginning with our children, are watching how we act in marriage. How do we talk to each other? How do we handle ourselves when not in each other's presence? How do we handle disagreements and challenges that come up in our relationship?

We realized our marriage provided a great way to minister to others. We have the opportunity to share our marriage with others. We could be the couple that said or did something to help restore hope in a couple or to encourage them as they are working to grow together.

Realizing this and having witnessed, up close and personal, the devastation that happens when a couple divorces, we were encouraged to be even better than just saying no to divorce. We said yes to allowing God to use us, our story, our hurts, pains, challenges, and successes for His glory in helping other couples.

Our prayer is that we encourage marriages, that we relate to their struggles that are typically similar to ours, and that we show them they can still make it and be happy through it all.

Will You Say No and Yes?

Your marriage is a ministry too. It may be a brand-new ministry, and it may only minister to you and your spouse right now, but it's not just about you, and if you agree to say no, you will see the opportunities to say yes. So, before we move onto the next part of the book, will you take the same stand Stephana and I took? Say no to divorce and yes to your marriage as a ministry.

On my blog I write and speak primarily to men. As a husband and father who felt like he didn't always do the best job of leading his family, my heart is for men who are similar to me in this way. So I want to challenge the husbands, specifically, before we move on.

Men, many times our wives will take the lead role in areas where we've left a void such as spiritual leadership or the education and enrichment of our kids. I want you men to step up so there is no void in these areas. Particularly within our marriages. Men, will you step up and assume your leadership role as husband? Will you be the champion God has called you to be when He blessed you with your wife?

I learned from my good friend, Kevin Bullard, of MarriageWorks.us, that you are automatically a champion once you get married.[2] One of the root meanings of the Hebrew word *husband* actually means "champion."[3]

So this means God has called us champs, and as such He expects us to love our wives like champs, just as Christ does the church. As the champion in our marriages, we have a twofold role: (1) defeat our rivals, and (2) fight on the behalf of our wives. We do this by caring and feeding her spiritually while we advance together against the enemies of our union.

If we were in the same room, I'd let out a loud battle cry to start the charge. So let this be your call, your battle cry to assume your designated role as husband, as champion in your marriage. The journey we are embarking on, the challenges we face, and the rings we'll wear won't always be easy or even always enjoyable. But the person we are fighting for and with is worth anything we have to go through on the way. Are you with me?

Chapter Three

The 7 Rings of Marriage— An Overview

"Coming together is a beginning; keeping together is progress; working together is success."
−Henry Ford

T his year my wife and I will celebrate our fifteenth wedding anniversary. We are both amazed at how far we've come. We've gone through a lot of ups and downs, and at times our relationship seemed downright dysfunctional. But through it all we can both say our marriage keeps growing and moving toward new levels, and today it's a healthy marriage.

We almost didn't make it and would have been on the wrong side of the divorce statistics. Our marriage was on the brink of failure before we even knew it—even before we had our first anniversary. We came into the marriage with plenty of individual baggage and bad relationship habits. And to add to those challenges, we had our first child before marriage, so you can see why we struggled.

Saving Our Marriage

The writing was on the wall for us to fail, but we didn't. A marriage class, counseling from the couple who taught the class, and a marriage retreat helped save our marriage. Since that rough start, we've remained happily together through all the stages of marriage, or what we like to call the *7 Rings of Marriage*. I'm talking financial issues, in-law issues, job loss, homelessness (twice!), trust issues, and a host of other challenges.

Having persevered through all of that, we now have confidence that we can withstand any challenge that presents itself in our marriage. I'm not saying these challenges are easy, but we now know what to expect because we've been through it. We've learned how to handle them in a way that keeps our relationship growing and essentially makes our marriage better. And through it all, a tremendous passion for marriage has developed, which is one of the reasons I'm writing this book today.

Saving Other Marriages

My hope in this book and all my writing and speaking is that I help the marriages of all couples who are like we once were. One of the first ways to help is by making sure you're aware of what to expect in marriage. When you know what to expect—when you know the *7 Rings of Marriage* successful married couples experience—then you'll be better prepared to navigate challenges in a way that helps your marriage rather than hurts it. So let's get started!

The 7 Rings of Marriage

1. *Engagement RING*

The beginning. Think vision—vision filled with hope, love, and possibility. You have no real clue of what challenges lie ahead, as it all seems blissful.

2. *Wedding RING*

The commitment. Think of your wedding day and saying, "I do." Your lives come together as one, and you can't think of anything better.

3. *DiscoveRING*

The real you. Think of pulling the covers off. After becoming one, sharing a home, and a lot of other stuff, you both begin to learn things you never knew about each other. This can be good and bad.

4. *PerseveRING*

The work. Think of the reward when you commit and work hard at something. This is why couples say, "Marriage takes work!" But you'll learn that work pays off in amazing ways.

5. *RestoRING*

The fixing. Think of healing and cleaning up. You both may have been hurt by each other at some point in your marriage, but your love prevails, and now you begin healing and making your marriage great.

6. *ProspeRING*

The goal. Think of happily ever after—of reaching your goal and realizing the vision you had when you were engaged. Now, after all you've been through, this is a reality.

7. MentoRING

The payback. Think of experiencing something great and wanting to share it. You want others to experience something similar. This drives you to help other couples that haven't experienced what you have.

Right at this moment it's safe to say that your marriage is "wearing" one of those rings. The first step is just recognizing which ring it is. Then you can begin to intentionally move from one ring to the next until your relationship is at its most mature stage and can remain a healthy marriage.*

* Visit my website for additional resources.

Chapter Four

Ring #1—Engagement RING

*"A relationship with God is the most
important relationship you can have."*

–Unknown

T hinking back to the first moment I knew I wanted to marry Stephana, I remember being filled with emotions. I can remember how nervous I was the day I proposed to her. I had a nervousness I had never experienced before. To this day I can't tell you exactly what I said, and to this day I don't know how she even understood what I said.

After she said yes, days after, the nervousness faded some, but still a ton of emotions followed from the time we were engaged to the time we said, "I do." My life was about to change in ways it had never changed before. I was committing to what would be the most important relationship I could have. Or so I thought.

Seeing Past the Surface

Early in our marriage I was bitten by a bug. The entrepreneurial bug. That infectious bite led me to launch our first business, a business investing in real estate. That bug would later be the catalyst for many experiences in our marriage, both good and bad.

In the five years we spent buying, rehabbing, managing, leasing, and selling real estate, I experienced and learned a lot. A few of those lessons were real estate specific and didn't have much application to other areas of my life, but quite a few have been helpful in other areas of my life, business, and even my marriage.

On a daily basis I would scour the city, both physically and digitally, for single-family homes that had some sort of problem. Once we purchased these homes, we'd hire contractors to fix the problems and get them ready for someone to live in. I looked at hundreds of houses per month and bought many of them over time. Every house and every rehab project was unique. Yes, we addressed some common, surface-level things like replacing the carpet, putting on a fresh coat of paint, and changing locks and doors, but once we got past the surface, things got tricky.

But those problems didn't deter us. In fact, the more problems a house had, the more excited I was about the house. More problems meant the potential for a lower purchase price (i.e. better deal). We could buy the house cheaper, which would enable us to receive a higher return on our investment.

There wasn't a problem we couldn't address, at least on the surface. Then I discovered that the big problems aren't surface level. I was somewhat naive to this because I was new to home ownership and maintenance. "Handyman" and my name are rarely listed in the same sentence or even the same paragraph. This discovery was the beginning of some of the biggest lessons I learned in real estate. (Note: when you hear an entrepreneur or investor say "lessons I learned," that usually means they lost money.)

We later learned some houses had foundation issues. Those houses may have looked good on the surface, but once we began to work on the house, we discovered issues that would take a lot more work than we anticipated. Issues with the foundation of a house can be repaired, but it is costly. Many times this cost was beyond our budget range, which meant our return would be significantly less if we even made a profit at all.

Those were painful but valuable lessons as we began to be more selective about how we invested our resources.

Laying the Foundation

Just like a house, our marriages have some sort of foundation. Some are solid as a rock and able to stand the test of time while others are like sand and easily blown away. Your "return" or the fulfillment you receive in marriage is directly related to the type of foundation you have.

If you are going to have a marriage that lasts and is fulfilling for both of you, you have to have a strong foundation. For some of you, this means laying the proper foundation at the beginning; for others it means restoring the foundation; while for others it means some major rehabilitation, or a complete tear down and rebuild are needed.

No matter which group you fall into, you should always work to strengthen your foundation. Not every property we came across that had foundation issues started that way. Some had great, well-laid foundations when built, but over time those foundations were weakened from other factors and a lack of care. Our marriage foundations can be weakened in the same way when we don't care for them.

The Engagement RING is where your marriage foundation is formed. Whether your relationship status is actually "engaged," or you've already said, "I do," does not matter. We are talking about the foundation of a lasting and fulfilling marriage. This is the beginning and the most important part of your journey. Your foundation determines how high your marriage can go, what it can stand on, as well as stand under. But don't be overly concerned if your foundation is shaky, made of straw, or has some cracks. Our foundation was weak from the beginning. However, over time we've been able to strengthen our marriage foundation and build from there.

When you realize you are wearing the Engagement RING, your focus should be on creating a solid foundation that will enable your marriage to survive "for better or for worse." When you are at the beginning, during engagement, or the beginning of a new season in your marriage, you have plenty of hope, possibility, and excitement. It is filled with so much of it that you may not realize, or remember, things aren't always smooth sailing. That's why you hear people say, "Love is blind." When you first fall in love with "the one," they can do no wrong. Your perspective is skewed so you miss a lot of things. That's why you need something to stand on.

Relational versus Transactional

I spent three years in commercial sales. We had clients that paid us a couple hundred dollars per year, and clients that paid us mid-five figures per year. That's a big difference in clients. That job was my first real sales job. While my real estate business did involve selling, what I did in real estate wasn't necessarily a sales job, at least not in this manner. So I studied sales and set out on a quest to learn what makes a successful salesperson. I learned one of the things that helps you become successful as a salesperson is becoming more relational instead of transactional. A relational salesperson will focus on building a long-term relationship and learning more about the customer so he or she can better serve them long-term. It involves some planning. Transactional salespeople focus on the point of sale and don't think very much about what will happen after the fact. Those large, five-figure accounts required some serious relational selling.

You can be relational or transactional during the Engagement RING just like a sales professional can. When you are transactional, you are focused on what appeals to you right now. The hope and excitement of what feels good now. You plan for the wedding, not the marriage. When you are relational, you understand you are going to spend a lot of time with this person, hopefully your entire life, and you learn as much as possible about that person, yourself, and how you will coexist together. You plan for the wedding *and* the marriage. There is a huge difference. You have to take the relational approach to anything new in your marriage. Think and plan about how it will fit into the grand scheme of your relationship, your family, your life, and your hopes and dreams. Doing so will result in the solid foundation you need to make your marriage last.

℞

I met Mark and Susan Merrill online in what was basically a job interview. The interview was more conversational than most, and I felt like I had known them for some time. I believe the first conversation was with Susan via a Google Hangout. The meeting was relaxed as we both video chatted from our respective homes. I was introduced to Mark and Susan by a good friend who plays a major role for the nonprofit they run.

One of the reasons the conversation with Susan, and soon after with Mark, went so well and it seemed like we had known each other for years was because I'd been following them and engaging with them online for some time already. I discovered Mark's work through All Pro Dad and his blog long before we connected on that Hangout. I saw someone in Mark that I could relate to as a husband and a father trying to lead his family.

Fast-forward a year or two, and we are all on another Google Hangout, including my wife this time. Instead of discussing my writing and the possibility of contributing content to All Pro Dad, we were discussing Mark and Susan's marriage for our *7 Rings of Marriage Web Show*. Stephana and I were so excited to have the opportunity to chat with them. By this time we'd both learned so much from them through my work with All Pro Dad as well as reading their blogs and books. What we learned from them while listening to their marriage journey was profound!

We already knew they had a long-lasting and truly intimate marriage, but what we didn't know was how they got there. We quickly learned one of the keys was the foundation they had set during the early years of their relationship. This foundation allowed everything else to flow from there. In comparison to our first year, it *was* smooth sailing.

When Stephana and I were married, our foundation was probably as weak as they come. We violated just about everything I write about and everything we speak and teach about when it comes to marriage "best practices." There was a time when I was ashamed to admit some of those things.

When people asked how many years we had been married and followed that up or preceded that question with, "How old are your kids?" I'd feel somewhat ashamed. I wasn't ashamed of our kids, my wife, or my marriage. My shame came from the fact that we, a Christian couple, had our first child before we were married. While that's not a big deal to some, I knew we didn't do things in order, and as you will see later, it made things harder for us in the early years of our marriage.

But on the surface, when you hear some snippets of our story you'd think "soul mates" and we had the perfect marriage. We grew up in the same small town. Our grandmothers grew up next door to each other, were best friends their entire lives, and even sat next to each other every Sunday at the church my wife and I both call our childhood church home. A mutual friend introduced us in high school, which was sort of the beginning of our relationship. I went away to college, only to move back to a new city where I knew two people: (1) a buddy of mine I played basketball with from the sixth grade through high school, and (2) my future wife.

While our story started in high school, it was far from the "marrying your high school sweetheart" story. When you got past the surface, our relationship's foundation was made up of unfaithfulness; premarital sex, which we called "hooking up": adulterous relationships; a child born out of wedlock; living together; a short engagement period; and an almost shorter marriage. All a different story from what it seems initially and vastly different from what we've learned we should have been doing and now teach to couples today. Stephana and I were married under some challenging circumstances. Those circumstances led to a first year and early part of our marriage that could have easily ended in divorce. In stark comparison, Mark and Susan started with an amazing foundation to their marriage. This foundation allowed them to grow a marriage they knew would last and has even taken them further than that, as they've spent decades helping others with their relationships, marriages, and families.

We're thankful we made it and have grown to the point where we can share our experiences, good and bad, to encourage other couples. However, I wish we had known how important a strong foundation was to our marriage, and what it looked like, before we were married. Did your mother ever tell you, "If you know better, you'll do better?" Knowing better would have definitely led to us doing better. It would have saved us from some of the problems we've faced and some that still have an impact on us today. Although we didn't know better initially, I'm glad once we did know better, and were exposed to important foundational things for our marriage, we began to change. Which ultimately led to building the foundation that saved our marriage.

In our conversation with Mark and Susan, they shared some practical things they did to build their foundation. The great part about what they did to create this foundation is no matter where you are in your marriage, you can begin to implement them today. Wearing the Engagement RING doesn't mean you have to be engaged. It means you are at a beginning point; it means your relationship could benefit from some foundational principles and actions that will help you move into the next phase in your marriage.

Friendship

Mark and Susan were friends before anything else. They hung out together, they hung out with groups of friends, and they spent a lot of time together. Yes, they found each other attractive, but this wasn't the driving force behind their relationship. They got to know each other in intimate ways that didn't include sex.

Being friends is foundational for your relationship. It sounds like common sense, and something that should obviously come with marriage, but it doesn't always. Sadly, many married couples today are not friends. My wife and I fell in that group at one time. We were roommates and business partners. (Our kids and our real estate were the products/services.) We were just "two ships passing in the night." Sometimes we didn't even like each other. Still sometimes today we don't "like" each other!

A marriage relationship void of friendship is a marriage relationship void of a foundation. It will crumble or topple over eventually. At best it'll be that rickety old structure nobody wants to live in, but you feel it's all you've got. How much fun and fulfillment will you get from that? Friendship is crucial, and friendship will be the seed that when planted results in a love that grows. Hang tight . . . we will come back to this theme of friendship throughout the book as it is one of the most important foundations to lay in your marriage.

Counsel

I like to say we got our "premarital counseling" after we were married. That makes a lot of sense, doesn't it? *Pre*, meaning "before," was done *post*, meaning "after." That was not a good choice, but in our defense we didn't know anything such as premarital counseling existed. Mark and Susan, on the other hand, were not only open to receiving counseling before marriage—they sought it out and embraced it. Mark even listened to the counsel of a close friend before he asked Susan to marry him. I, on the other hand, didn't talk to anybody about it except my dad when I asked him to go with me to pick out the engagement ring. And to be totally transparent I probably only asked him to come because I may have needed some financial help.

My point is, I didn't seek any type of counseling from anybody. Mark was eager to find and follow the counsel of those who could help. Our marriage started off in need of a foundation repair. Mark and Susan's started off in an amazing way, preparing them to launch into their lives and purposes together.

Similar to the friendship part of your relationship's foundation, counseling isn't only reserved for those getting engaged or those in trouble. If you're years into your marriage, it is not too late. As I said, our premarital counseling happened about a year after we were married. We learned what we should have learned before marriage, and it wasn't too late. It's never too late to seek the advice of someone who is wiser than you in any area, especially for your marriage.

Our premarital counseling came in the form of the class we took together at our church. In that class we learned the who, the what, the how, and a bunch of other things related to marriage. And we learned about each other, why we were struggling, and were forewarned of other potential issues that may arise. I'm thankful for our "pre/postmarital" counseling. It helped us intentionally lay the foundation we neglected before.

Prayer

Stephana and I pray for and with each other now but not as consistently as we would like. We both believe prayer is a privilege that is powerful in our lives, and know it is something we must do. It wasn't always that way. If Stephana had asked me to pray with her years ago, it would have been uncomfortable. I think it would have been the same for her if I asked her to pray with me. We probably would have thought something was drastically wrong, somebody had a grave sickness, or something along those lines. As people who believe in Jesus Christ and believe that the "prayer of a righteous man availeth much" (James 5:16 KJV), it would seem that prayer in marriage would be a given. But it wasn't.

It wasn't always a given in Mark and Susan's foundation-building season of their relationship either. In fact, the lack of praying together resulted in the end of their relationship for a short time prior to them even getting married. Susan was advised through someone she received counsel from that if they were going to be in a committed relationship then they should be praying together. Mark, probably like many men at that stage, felt uncomfortable with praying together. Susan didn't understand why that would be the case and truly believed prayer must be a part of their relationship if they were committed. So she ended the relationship, and they almost never made it to an actual engagement or marriage.

Wow! That is powerful to me. She knew prayer was so important and so imperative that if it was absent it'd be better to not be together. Fortunately, after prayer became a part of their relationship, God brought Mark and Susan back together. Then engagement and marriage followed. That's a stance I want to take in all areas of my life. Her decision to settle for nothing less than the best in him, from him, and in their relationship is something for us to take seriously.

Praying with your spouse is vital in building the right foundation in your marriage as well as continuing to grow together. But praying together is one of the hardest things to start doing. It can be uncomfortable, it can be weird, it can even be scary. But it doesn't have to be. Whether you have been praying together for a while or you have never even considered it, here are seven ways to help you pray more consistently and enrich your prayer times with your spouse.

1. *Choose a time but be flexible.* I believe what doesn't get scheduled doesn't get done. Choosing a time to come together will help you get it done. But flexibility is important. If you miss, it's okay, just get right back on track. Likewise, if either of you feel the need to pray at any given moment, don't decline because it's not at the scheduled time. There's never a bad time to pray.

2. *Pray alone before praying together.* Sometimes you need a supernatural act just to get you in the room to pray with your spouse. James 4:2 says, "You do not have because you do not ask." Ask God for strength, courage, the right words, whatever you need to go into your prayer room with your spouse.

3. *Thank God and praise Him for your spouse.* Break down any barriers between you and your spouse or between you and God. Thank Him for who He is. Praise Him for blessing you with your spouse.

4. *Use Scripture for your prayers.* Sometimes we just don't know what to pray, or we are afraid our prayers are based on our own selfish desires and motives. The best way to ensure that isn't the case is to pray God's Word. Use Scripture in your prayers. Pray that He "will not leave you or forsake you" and "that all things work together" for good in your marriage (Deut. 31:6; Rom. 8:28).

5. *Write a prayer and read it.* Sometimes you have specific things you are troubled by or specific things you want to share your praise about. Write them down. There is nothing wrong with taking your time to write out your prayer and reading it during your prayer time.

6. *Start short.* Do not, I repeat, do not turn your couple's prayer time into a thirty-minute prayer call. At least not initially. Keep it short at first. And as you both strengthen your prayer muscles (and your knees can take it), feel free to pray on.

7. *Show some affection.* Just about every time we pray together, I kiss my wife, hug her, or show some sort of affection. Prayer is intimate, revealing, and personal. Don't pray and get up like you just left a business meeting. I will be transparent and say that sometimes our intimate prayer time leads to another type of intimate time together. So don't be surprised at the power of your prayer.

Prayer is of utmost importance in your relationship before you get married and after you get married. It will be an intricate component of the building or rebuilding of your foundation. You may need help getting started, but no matter what, don't forsake praying for and with your spouse at any point in your marriage. We will come back to prayer many times throughout this book. It is *the* game changer of game changers!

The Cornerstone

One thing that is vitally important in building construction is the cornerstone. The cornerstone is the first stone set in the construction of a masonry foundation. It is vital because all other stones will be set in reference to this stone, which determines the position of the entire structure.

So the entire structure centers around, or depends on, the cornerstone. Without the proper cornerstone the whole building can be thrown out of whack. Mark and Susan found their cornerstone and believe it was the most important thing they had together.

Their cornerstone was God, and they both agreed to center their friendship and relationship on Him. Everything they said and did was set in reference to Him. They didn't always agree to everything, but they agreed to this.

We've done the same thing. Once we learned that marriage was God-created and He made it to function best by following His principles, we've been setting everything else in reference to this. Maybe you have been setting your marriage on another cornerstone. Perhaps it is how the movies portray marriage and love. Or what your parents showed or taught you based on their relationship. It could be your friends. Or maybe there is no cornerstone to your marriage at all. None of that matters now. Find the Cornerstone that has led to an amazing marriage for Mark and Susan, as well as Stephana and me. You can start with history's first marriage, which began in Genesis 2, and go from there. God initiated this first marriage by forming Eve out of Adam's rib. They were literally, and physically, one with each other. Genesis 2:24 says, "This is why a man leaves his father and mother and bonds with his wife, and they become one flesh."

Without this Cornerstone you won't pray together, you'll doubt counseling, and your friendship will probably remain surface level. But with this Cornerstone everything will be properly set, and your foundation will be strong enough to last and stable enough to build a fulfilling marriage.

Strengthening the Foundation

The main reason we didn't go to work on building a good foundation for our marriage early on, or while wearing the Engagement RING, was because we just didn't know. If you don't know, you don't know. Hopefully by now you understand how crucial it is to have the right foundation for your marriage. But knowing isn't enough. We have to translate that knowledge into practical ways to strengthen our foundation.

Stephana and I are fast learners but slow doers. Thus our marriage functioned for years with a straw-strength foundation similar to the first of the three little pigs. We were blown around by the slightest wind that came our way.

My slow doing comes from wanting everything to be perfect first, before moving forward with action. My wife's slow doing comes from wanting results immediately but not always pressing through if they don't show. So, if it wasn't laid out and perfect ahead of time, I'd procrastinate on it. And Stephana would be ready to call it a day the minute it didn't feel right or provide the results she expected. That means it can take us a while to get some consistency.

It did take us a while, and we are still working on it, but our foundation has improved by leaps and bounds, and our marriage has followed suit. Some things will tip you off as to the strength of your foundation. Here are a few of them:

- You repeatedly get tripped up by the same issues.
- You have a hard time coming together spiritually.
- You are drained versus energized when in each other's company.
- External circumstances easily send you over the edge while your spouse's pain doesn't always move you.

- You don't know what to talk about when together.

The points above don't make up an exhaustive list, nor are they scientific. However, they do relate to your marriage's foundation, as they will be directly impacted when you take practical steps to strengthen your foundation.

We've experienced them, and still experience them on occasion, but nowhere near like we used to. It's ironic that prior to our getting married, or even officially dating, we considered ourselves pretty good friends. Then after dating and especially after marriage, that friendship seemed to dissolve. During our really good friend days we had great conversations. It was great because it was open and honest. When something went down in either one of our lives, we were able and willing to share about it. At some point after we became more than friends, there was a change. That change was a direct result of me and my unfaithful lifestyle, prior to getting married, which was eventually uncovered.

I created a culture of dishonesty in our relationship that lasted for years, and even after I changed my behavior, the damage was done. This damage resulted in a lack of trust from Stephana. It got to the point where we weren't able to talk to each other. Conversations were weird and guarded. She had been hurt and wasn't about to open up and risk being hurt like that again. I knew the pain I caused and felt any wrong statement could bring that right back to the surface.

This was something that stayed with us for years into our marriage. I can't tell you exactly when we grew past it, but I can tell you some of the things we did that helped.

Not in a Million Years

As I mentioned in chapter 2, in those marriage courses and conversations we had with our marriage mentors, we learned we had to eliminate one thing in our marriage. That one thing was the option of getting a divorce or separating. As long as divorce was an option, then divorce was a possibility. We were encouraged to take a hard-line approach with this. To not even speak the word, whether that was in anger, in jest, or any other fashion. It was completely outlawed in our house. About the only time we spoke of it was when we had conversations with other couples about eliminating it as an option in their marriages.

I can say without a doubt that this was the biggest thing that kept our marriage together in the early years. It gave us both the assurance that we were not going to be left alone, but it also gave us a sense of accountability that we had to be there, and we couldn't do anything stupid to put us in a situation where we would be tempted to make divorce an option. But it took more than just saying, "Divorce is not an option." We had to have a deep down conviction to live that out. That conviction came from our Cornerstone. Our conviction comes from God's feelings toward divorce, as spoken in Malachi 2:16 (NASB), "For I hate divorce." That's all I needed to hear. If He hated it, then I wanted to take the same stance. That became bigger than our feelings were at any given moment. It became bigger than someone telling us to take divorce off the table. Our desire to please God—or, better yet, our desire not to let Him down—became a foundational part of our marriage.

Without Compromise

Just about every church, Christian marriage ministry, or counselor will teach the "divorce is not an option" principle. Most will teach the basic same principles, similar to how people who teach money management teach you to spend less than you earn. Spending less than you earn is common sense, but for some reason not everybody does it. I've always wondered why. I've wondered why we can get some information that appears to be sound and helpful but go a totally different way. Total transparency here—we are guilty at times in our finances. But I'm happy to say we are less guilty when it comes to similar instances in our relationship.

We believe without compromise that divorce should not be an option. We believe without compromise that the husband is the head of the wife, not as a superior being but an equal being with the responsibility to cover her. We believe without compromise that the wife is to submit to her husband as she does to the Lord. We believe without compromise that we are to leave anything that prevents us from coming together as one, including our fathers and mothers. We never tried to "beat the system" in these areas. We fell short many times, still do, but our aim once we received these truths was to live them out as best we could. And never give up in doing so.

You cannot waiver in this area if you want a strong foundation. If you build one part of the foundation with bricks and the other with straw because building with straw was easier, or because somebody else built theirs with straw, or you just feel like it, then get ready to get huffed and puffed and blown down. I don't think stubbornness is necessarily a good thing, or a secret "fruit of the Spirit," but boy it has served me well in some areas. This one in particular. When I receive something that reveals itself as true, it is hard for me to change my mind. I'll often mess it up in my pursuit, but that stubborn pursuit will not stop. You have to have a stubbornness like this in regard to these principles when it comes to your marriage.

Quantity and Quality Time

We've been approached by other couples and friends who've said to us: "We never see you two apart. When we see one, we see the other." I'm not sure if we really paid attention to this fact, but we were together a lot, still are, although not as much due to our kids' schedules. Through this we've gotten a lot of quantity time. It wasn't always quality time, but it was time together. We didn't realize it at the time, but spending so much time together created an attachment that would not have been there had we done more things apart. This actually started before we were married, even before we were "officially" dating.

My wife and I grew up in the same town, which is about an hour's drive from where we live now, in Indianapolis. As young twenty-somethings, whenever a holiday rolled around, we'd go home to see our parents, grandparents, and attend family gatherings. We'd often call or connect with each other while in our hometown for the weekend or holiday. At some point we'd reach out to see when the other was driving back. Then we'd coordinate to follow each other back to Indianapolis. Sometimes we would talk on the phone the entire drive back. It was a way of spending time together. Eventually those trips grew to spending a lot more time with each other on those visits home as well.

We would be regular guests at each other's houses and family functions. My mother-in-law used to fill her refrigerator with the things she noticed I liked. She still has a knack for observing and giving the best, most timely, and needed gifts. One Thanksgiving, while we were sharing what we were thankful for on video camera, my mom decided to share how much she would love to have Stephana as her daughter-in-law. I was twenty-four years old at the time and still single! So you can imagine my thoughts and Stephana's! They noticed how we always found ourselves together and apparently saw something more, or at least were hoping for something more.

Through all the time we spent together before dating, during dating, and especially after marriage and kids, it helped us to feel more and more comfortable with each other. There were challenges, especially when my unfaithfulness was exposed, but spending a large quantity of time together helped us through that challenge as well. (Let me interject this really quick—a lack of trust should not be a reason to spend quantity time together, but at least Stephana knew I wasn't out doing something I should not be doing.) We enjoyed ourselves. We watched people and sometimes had inside jokes about what we saw. Over time it helped us to grow more fond of each other.

If you want to strengthen your foundation, spend time together. Don't take trips alone unless you have to. Don't do more girls' nights and guys' nights than date nights. Try to find hobbies or activities you can do together. Quality time will not come without quantity time. You are fooling yourself if you think quality time will happen auto-matically. It comes through time spent together, good times and bad times. Through it all an understanding and appreciation of each other grows. So, when you are working on your foundation, spend as much time as you possibly can together, even when it doesn't seem necessary.

At the beginning of any new season in your relationship, you may find yourself wearing the Engagement RING. This is your opportunity to create a foundation that will serve your marriage well for years. Don't neglect your foundation. Don't plan for the wedding (the event) and not plan for your marriage (your life). Develop your friendship through quality time spent together and open, honest communication. Lean on the wisdom and experiences of others, which can help you form the habits and principles that will guide your marriage. Most important, establish a Cornerstone, a relationship with Jesus Christ, that will serve as the center of everything you do in your marriage. You can build a skyscraper-sized marriage when you do.

Here are some questions to help you while wearing the Engagement RING:

1. What preparation have you done to get married (i.e., pre-marital counseling, conversations about finances, family planning, household management, etc.)?
2. How will this preparation or lack thereof impact your marriage?

Chapter Five

Ring #2—Wedding RING

*"Happy marriages begin when we marry the ones we love,
and they blossom when we love the ones we marry."*

–Tom Mullen

S everal years ago my nephew had a special friend in his life (to us grown folk, she was known as a girlfriend). In the middle of a conversation he and I were having, I said the "G" word (girlfriend). He quickly refuted the fact that she was his girlfriend. So, being the good uncle, who is more like a big brother, I asked him, "So, what makes a girl your girlfriend or not?" The answer I received made no sense at all. He basically talked around it to the point I think we were both confused. Of course I pressed further, only to find out that she was not his "girlfriend" because they had not called each other that yet. They had not said those words to or about each other; yet they dated just like a girlfriend and boyfriend do. Makes sense, huh? No, it doesn't. Unless you are a teenage boy early in your dating years or you are a grown man about to go from engaged to married.

Something about making a commitment to a relationship does something to us guys, no matter what age we are. I remember two of my best friends, one I went to high school with and another I knew in college. Both were the first guys to get married out of our respective circle of friends. My high school buddies were shocked, and so were my college buddies. We couldn't understand. How could these guys make that type of commitment? What were they thinking? Was something wrong? Had they been tricked? (Yes, that question did come up!)

For some reason getting married can be scary and confusing for us guys as we think about going from having only one person to answer to, that being ourselves, to having another person to answer to, no matter how much we love them. But it shouldn't be that way. The commitment I made to Stephana is the second greatest commitment I've made in my life, second only to my commitment to follow Christ.

Commitment is what wearing the Wedding RING is all about. It's one of the most exciting times in your relationship, but when you don't know what to expect, or what all comes with that commitment, it can be scary. It's kind of like public speaking. Fear of public speaking surpasses even the fear of death. I've gone from someone who feared public speaking, like people fear death, to someone who speaks on a regular basis. I've learned the more prepared I am to speak, the less fear and nervousness I have. I want to prepare you and help you handle the commitments in your relationship to help reduce and even eliminate any fear or confusion you may have.

It's not uncommon today for couples to function like a husband and wife should function by living together, without committing to marrying each other. It seems more couples are choosing "shacking up," cohabiting, or whatever you call it, versus getting married. It's a shame because without commitment you can't realistically do the things you should be doing at that stage. Stephana and I were one of the couples that chose to live together without the commitment of marriage. (As I already mentioned, we did almost everything wrong, or backwards, in the beginning.)

The first true commitment that took place in our relationship was the commitment to raise our daughter together. That's what led to our decision to live together, although we weren't married or even engaged at the time. This was the time when we should have been dreaming, hoping, and making plans for our future, but we weren't. We couldn't. There was too much uncertainty. Will we be together in the future? Will this work out? Am I going to be a single parent? It's amazing the impact our choices have on our futures, especially when we do things out of order.

We went from not really being exclusive in our relationship, to pregnant, to cohabitating, to committing to a church home (the best choice we made during this time), to engaged, to married in a matter of about eighteen months. Those are all things that are supposed to be dreamed of and planned for over time when you first enter the Wedding RING stage of your relationship. Many of our problems were caused by skipping steps, which came from our being unaware. Remember, if you know better, you'll do better.

Wet Cement

As a kid, did you ever come across a sidewalk that had fresh, wet cement? Or maybe your family built a new house or did concrete work on your driveway or property? As a kid you may have done the mischievous thing—grabbed a stick and wrote your name or something while the cement was still wet. As an adult maybe you wrote the date your home was built, as a kind of memorial.

You knew if you got whatever it was you wanted to write in that cement in time, while it was still wet, and nobody came and smoothed it over, it would be there forever. That's what happens when you make an imprint in wet cement.

My good friend Kevin Bullard says the first six to nine months of your marriage is like wet cement. Similar to writing your name as a kid, or writing a significant date as an adult in wet cement, the imprints made during that time period, if not smoothed over or changed, will last. For your marriage, after roughly six to nine months, those imprints will be set in stone and will more than likely last throughout the duration of your marriage. The words you say, the actions you take, and the course you set will have a major impact going forward.[1]

This is ideal for fully committing, dreaming together, and laying out the course for your marriage and your life as one. These are exciting times, and if there is going to be something that follows you or remains throughout your marriage, you want it to be something that energizes you and brings life. You get to test out those things from that foundation you laid during the Engagement Ring. Later on things will get tough, really tough in your marriage, and what you've written in the wet cement can give you the inspiration and even the courage to keep you growing together and moving forward. Every one of the 7 Rings will help prepare you for subsequent rings and experiences you'll encounter in marriage. Don't miss out on your opportunity to create a significant imprint on your marriage during the Wedding Ring, when it's still wet cement.

A Shared Vision

I talked earlier about forgetting everything you thought you knew about marriage. You want to clean the slate of your previous ideals and notions. Once you've committed to doing that, you are free to create your own shared vision. We didn't do enough of this in the early stages of our marriage. I became a big goal setter a year or so into our marriage, but most of my goal setting and the vision I could see was painted by me alone. I then wanted Stephana to buy in or accept without much of her input. This was a failed strategy. God brought us together not just for me to say this is how it's going to be but for us to pray, discuss, and jointly plan how it is going to be.

Only in recent years has Stephana been as engaged in the vision for our family as I have. Prior to this she rarely objected unless it was truly something crazy or off-the-wall. And I was definitely capable and skilled enough to come up with crazy, off-the-wall stuff. But the shared vision for our marriage wasn't a reality.

One of the problems was "our vision" was based on things that excited me but weren't necessarily exciting or engaging to her. While we shared and embraced certain foundational principles, we weren't always on the same page with how it played out, how we'd get to our destination, or what our relationship would look like in the future.

Since we recognized God's plans for us are directly linked to each other, our prayer, discussions, and the things we are working on are more energizing. They aren't always easy, but working toward something with our spouses brings excitement to our marriages. This goes for all areas. If we did something a certain way in my household growing up and we adopt that for no other reason than that's the way it was done during my upbringing, then the potential for both people to fully embrace it is not that great.

However, when you work together to create something, to determine how your relationship and family will function, that produces something you both can get behind. It belongs to both of you, similar to the feeling you have when you have kids together. Those kids are so special because your love and the fact that you came together as one created them. It's no different for parents who adopt children. They may not have conceived together, but they planned, prayed, and went through the adoption process to make it happen. At this point in your relationship, one of the most important things you can do is come together and set your sights on where, how, and what your marriage will do, be, and have. It's part of the joys of the Wedding RING.

It doesn't matter if you have the model marriage, your marriage is on the brink of divorce, or you are newlyweds or seasoned marriage vets. You can always improve your marriage. But it won't just happen. You have to make it happen. So, what is your plan to make it happen? What is your plan to improve your marriage?

We Plan Everything

Have you gone on vacation with your family? I bet you planned that vacation. Have you taken a road trip? You probably mapped it out or put it in your GPS. Are you an entrepreneur? At some point you created a business plan, or at least were told you needed to. Trying to get out of debt? You are probably following the Dave Ramsey plan or some similar debt elimination plan. And I bet you had a plan for your wedding!

The point is, we plan for *everything* in our lives. But I have yet to hear couples consistently say they have a plan for their marriage. We have been taught in order to have success, we must plan. You know the saying . . .

"Fail to plan, plan to fail!"

Perhaps that could be the reason so many marriages fail. There was no plan to have a lasting, loving, and amazing marriage.

Do you want to improve your marriage? If you want a better marriage, you have to invest in it. You have to know that you want it to grow, to last, and to be fulfilling to both you and your spouse. Once you decide that, which should have been decided before saying, "I do," you then have to be intentional.

Once you and your spouse are in agreement, it is time to start designing a plan that will lead to your ideal marriage and lead toward that "happily ever after" you hoped for on your wedding day.

Your Marriage Success Plan

On June 16, 2016, I will have been married to my wife for fifteen years. We have big plans for our marriage and our family. You should too. Here are some essentials you should include in your marriage success plan.

1. *Marriage Goals.* What do you want to happen in your marriage? Where do you want to go? What do you want to accomplish together? Write it down. Studies show that writing your goals down increases your chances of achieving them.
2. *Mission, Vision, and Purpose.* God brought you together for a purpose bigger than you. Begin to seek it out. How will other people be positively impacted by your union in a way that neither of you could have done individually?
3. *Marriage Mentors.* The Bible cautions us about making plans without seeking counsel. Proverbs 15:22 says, "Plans fail when there is no counsel, but with many advisers they succeed." Your marriage needs regular counseling or mentoring, which will give you insight from the experiences of other great marriages.
4. *Regular Date Nights.* This is like food for your marriage. Without a commitment to continued courting, activities, and time alone, it will be hard to thrive. Our bodies need food. Our marriages need dates.
5. *Annual Big Vacations (Alone).* Seeing and experiencing different things together is like a breath of fresh air. Getting away from the norm can clear your mind and provide an escape allowing you to focus on each other. Plus it is just fun!
6. *Small Weekend Getaways.* Like the big vacations these are good for removing all distractions. They could be in the form of a marriage retreat, a shopping trip, or just quiet time together.
7. *A Couple to Mentor.* Just like having kids, having another couple to teach and share your experiences with will cause you to be more accountable and to seek to learn more in hopes of improving your marriage and theirs. The Dead Sea is dead because water only flows in, and nothing flows out. Mentoring serves as your way to pour your blessings into another couple.

8. *Married Friends in the Same Season.* Sometimes in marriage you feel as if you are the only couple going through your particular circumstances. You may feel your mentors and mentees don't understand. Having married friends similar to your stage will prove this wrong and provide opportunities for you to relate to others along the same journey.

9. *Marriage Exit Strategy.* I am not talking about divorce. Divorce should come up only once—in premarital counseling when you both agree never to mention it, consider it, or entertain it at all. Your exit strategy is "until death do us part."

10. *Boundaries.* You should agree never to do certain things and never to cross certain lines. A boxing match has rules; MMA fighting has rules (I think). Even when you are disagreeing, these boundaries need to be respected.

11. *Leaving a Legacy.* How will you pass on your family name? Kids? How will you impact the next generation of marriages? Ministry? Make a plan to be a blessing to future generations of marriages.

12. *Financial and Fitness Plans.* Your bodies will not always look the same as they did on your wedding day. Hopefully your finances will not either. Make a plan to be as healthy physically and fiscally as you can. Your spouse could be your exercise partner. Your financial plan will determine some of your ability to do some of the other aspects of your plan.

13. *Making Your Marriage a Priority.* Pour yourself into your marriage. Never stop learning your spouse. Never stop trying to improve your marriage. Read books, attend seminars and retreats, subscribe to blogs, talk to couples you respect. Spend time and money on improving your marriage.

I will revisit many of these ideas in later chapters, but for now understanding the need to have a plan for your family is of utmost importance. Family is the foundation to many things in society. Your marriage is the foundation of your family. Pour a solid foundation with a great marriage success plan; then give all you have to make sure your plan succeeds.

Wholehearted Commitment

When I describe the Wedding RING season of marriage to couples, I use these words: "This is the walking around the house with nothing on, feelin' good stage!" I tell them to enjoy this season, as you may not get to experience something like it again in your marriage. Many couples, not all, are young in age while wearing the Wedding RING. You don't have children yet. For those of you who didn't move in together, or have sexual relations prior to marriage, you get to experience it for the first time. For those of you that did, you get to experience sex completely free of any guilt. There is no other time like it!

My wife and I didn't get to fully experience the Wedding RING season in this manner. Our daughter was ten months old when we were married, and while we don't regret having her one bit, it would have been nice to enjoy a "traditional" Wedding RING season. It was a little unfair, to her and to us, as we weren't always able to give her our best because we were still trying to figure everything out ourselves. We didn't know how to give her our best yet. And I'm not just talking about parenting but figuring out how to commit to our relationship and marriage and everything that comes with both. So, when you say, "I do," and enter this season, choose joy in all circumstances and savor the time. The time goes by way faster than you want, just like most good things.

At some point it will be difficult to remember the things that happened while wearing the Wedding RING. You will go from your heart racing every time you see her to your blood boiling every time you see her. You'll go from experiencing what it feels like to be head over heels in love to secretly, but ashamedly, wishing your spouse would fall and topple head over heels. You'll also have to make some hard choices that you may not understand at the time. One of them is how to handle old friendships and old flames. In the age of Facebook, it is easier than ever to locate an old boyfriend or girlfriend and casually "see what they are up to." If you are truly going to commit to your relationship, and leave and cleave as Genesis 2:24 says, then you must decommit to other relationships and attachments.

One of the most important things you can do at this stage, besides enjoy the fun and excitement of new love, is to come together in all aspects of your marriage. Your goals, your planning, your money, your stuff, your bodies, and even your passwords. Some things are easier than others. You want to share a home, but you don't necessarily want to share everything in it. You want some affection when you're in need but not always when you're not in the mood. You want him to update his Facebook status to married, but you don't necessarily want him to have access to your account.

Many couples have problems later on because they only partially commit during this part of their marriage. The Wedding RING is about wholehearted commitment to each other as a couple. Remember, you are no longer two individuals; you are now one.

Celebration

Much of the Wedding RING phase is cause for celebration. The wedding ceremony, a new life together, perhaps a new house, new town—and, of course, there is the physical celebration. Making love is a celebration for you and your spouse. Making love in marriage is the result of you and your spouse connecting, then celebrating your connection. So, if making love isn't feeling like much of a celebration to you or your wife, then maybe you are missing a connection or two.

Stephana and I attend an annual marriage retreat, and at one in particular we learned a tremendously valuable lesson. Since that retreat our relationship began clicking on a much greater level. That big takeaway was viewing sex as a celebration. Celebrations are fun. Celebrations are rewarding. Celebrations come after something has been accomplished. There is no closer, more intimate way to connect with another human being than having sex. What a great idea God had when He made us with the physical ability to celebrate like this! However, there are some prerequisites. That physical celebration will never happen the way it should without some other nonphysical connections first. Many wives are probably nodding their heads yes in confirmation of that statement.

The speaker at the marriage conference said when a man and woman connect on three levels the physical celebration of sex will naturally follow. Fellas, if you make these three connections, you will "celebrate" as much as you can handle. In fact, you may have to take a break from celebrating. That is a great problem to have.

Are there marriages that have sex even when they haven't made the three connections? Yes. Are there marriages that have connected in one or two areas but not the third and still have regular sex? I'm sure there are. But the sex may not be the celebration both husband and wife are looking for.

Here are the three connections you need to make to regularly celebrate with sex in your marriage:

1. *Connect emotionally.* Sex is more risky for a woman than a man. During sex a woman is vulnerable, both physically and emotionally. Husbands, if you have not made an emotional connection, it becomes harder for your wife to be willing to celebrate physically. When your wife feels emotionally safe and secure, she will more likely want to celebrate. Fellas, make your wife feel emotionally safe. Help her want to celebrate.

2. *Connect intellectually.* What makes your spouse tick? What are her likes and dislikes? Get in your spouse's head. When you connect on this level, you will have more intimate conversations. You both will reveal more to each other. A level of transparency will come. You will even be able to talk about sex. Fellas, you won't be shooting "blindly" hoping you are

doing things right. You'll know because you both feel connected enough to discuss it.

3. *Connect spiritually.* I don't know where you are in your relationship with Christ. But I know my marriage would not have made it this far without Christ being first in our relationship. Connecting at this level is essential. Prayer for and with your wife tears down any barriers. Try praying for your spouse when you are mad at him or her. The more you pray for your spouse, the more that anger goes away. Connecting spiritually brings down walls and makes it that much easier to celebrate.

Maybe your marriage and sex life are all you both hoped for. Would you agree that connecting on those levels has been a huge reason? Maybe your marriage and sex life are suffering and you have nothing to celebrate. If so, work on connecting emotionally, intellectually, and spiritually. Then start poppin' bottles because the celebration will soon follow.

Love Letters

Your words can speak life or death to your marriage. However, some of what you say verbally can be forgotten over time. But words you put on paper can last forever. When was the last time you wrote a love letter to your husband or wife?

Recently, my wife and I attended a marriage conference. During the conference we were asked to write love letters to each other. But not just random "Roses are red, violets are blue" type stuff. We were provided a guide to help us put into perspective our marriage, each other, and God's role in our marriage. The results we got from doing this were amazing! Every married couple should take the time to do it as well. Below is a guide to help you write a love letter to your spouse.

1. *Pray.* Before you sit down to write, kneel down to pray. God created marriage, and He should be included in all aspects. Thank God for your spouse and give praise for his or her good attributes. Confess that you haven't been the best husband or wife you can be. Admit any negative feelings or thoughts, and ask God to help you with them. Men, ask God to help you see her as the beautiful woman He created. Ladies, ask God to help you see him as a man after God's own heart. Finally, pray about your roles and ask for help in fulfilling them.

2. *Write it down.* After praying, it is time to write. Write your thoughts in letter form. Think back to when you first met and what attracted you to him or her. Think of how you now complement each other. Think of the areas you have let your spouse down and areas in which you need to improve. Think of your commitment in all these areas from this point forward and list some ways you will fulfill this commitment.

3. *Share and discuss.* Read your love letters to each other. Discuss them, express the commitments you made during your prayer time, and pray together again.

Here is the love letter I wrote my wife to hopefully give you some ideas . . .

Hey Babe,

From the first time we met, you've always had this gentle, kind, and caring spirit that really made you attractive to me. You still have that same spirit, and it still attracts me today. It doesn't matter what happens, your default response is gentleness, kindness, and care.

God is amazing in His plan and His perfect will. We are similar in some areas but very different in others. I'm the planner, deliberator, and the one who takes forever before taking action. You, on the other hand, love surprises and spontaneity. Two of me would be boring and would never get around to doing anything. Two of you would set off only to look up later and have no idea where we are. But one of you and one of me is perfect.

I have done some crazy things, some silly things, and some outright stupid things. But you never wavered in the respect and support you had for me. I'm not sure any other woman would or could have put up with me and all that comes with being married to me.

I know I haven't always done the best job of loving and leading you. My desire is to do much better. One way I plan to do so is by not putting anyone or anything ahead of you, except God. I haven't always done that; I admit it is wrong and ask for your forgiveness.

My prayer is to love you more than you know you can be loved and to lead in a way that makes you excited to follow. I won't stop trying until I do.

I love you!

What do you hope to happen in your relationship by taking time out to go through this love-letter exercise? I believe your spouse will love you for your transparency and love you even more exactly as you are. God created a perfect match for you, and it's something to be thankful for.

Best Friends = Best Marriages

I mentioned in the previous chapter that setting the foundation of friendship for your marriage is important in the Engagement Ring. It's also vital in the Wedding Ring phase. *If you are going to spend the rest of your life with someone, you should have a foundation of friendship.*

We can all agree with that, and probably most of us can say it was true of our relationship before marriage. But what about best friends? Is your spouse your best friend? And do you want to be best friends with your spouse?

What are the qualities of best friends? For starters, best friends love each other no matter what, and they are *not judgmental.* You can be you and don't have to worry about a thing. There is *a sense of security* that you can share anything on your mind, anything about yourself and your feelings, and it is safe. Best friends have a foundation of *truth and trust.* Best friends *know you.* Your likes and dislikes, your habits, both good and bad. And of course, best friends *love spending time together.*

Why is having your spouse as your best friend so great for your marriage? When you are faced with a challenge, there is nobody you'd want to help you face it more than your best friend, your "homie," your "bestie," your "ace." When your spouse is that person, you have someone rolling with you at all times! It can be you and your spouse against the world, and you are cool with that!

Marriage is not a boyfriend/girlfriend relationship you can swap out for another. It is for life! You will do anything you can to prevent something coming between you and your best friend. That is a great security blanket. And if you are going to spend every day with someone, you want it to be someone you enjoy spending time with.

Are you and your spouse friends but not best friends? Here are some ways you can move to being best friends. Remember the thing about quantity time leading to quality time? It's so important that it's necessary to mention again. Having a family and/or a career means having a lot going on in your life. Be *intentional* about spending quality time alone. *Be transparent.* Let your spouse in. Sometimes in marriage we let our "boys" or our girlfriends in but not our spouses. The person you let in is the person that has the potential to be your best friend. Most important, begin to *put your spouse's needs above yours.* That is the best competition you can have in marriage. The competition to meet each other's needs ahead of your own.

Whether you and your spouse share a best-friend relationship or not, it is something to be desired. And it is something you can grow into. I encourage you to look honestly at your relationship. Work on becoming best friends together! It is well worth it! We'll cover more on becoming, and staying, best friends in the next chapter.

Preventative Marriage Counseling

Should you seek marriage counseling when things are "good" in your marriage? I mean, if it ain't broke, don't fix it, right? I'm not so sure. Just as there are no perfect people, there are no perfect marriages. Unfortunately, many couples come to this realization too late.

Marriage counseling. Those words scream "major problems," a "bad marriage," or "the brink of divorce." Marriage counseling is not something couples post on Facebook like they do their trip to the islands.

Marriage counseling seems to come with a stigma. A stigma that says you don't know what you are doing in your relationship, and one, if not both of you, is messed up. Well, that is true. Both of you are messed up and are messing up your marriage! Which is why your marriage *always* needs fixing.

While my wife and I went to counseling early in our marriage because we were having issues, there was a time we went to "unofficial" marriage counseling. After meeting and becoming friends with Clarence and Brenda Shuler, the keynote speakers at a marriage conference we attended, we agreed to keep in touch. This led to Clarence and I having phone conversations, to discussing our marriage and work, to eventually setting up a counseling session.

Keep in mind, we weren't having "major problems," divorce was nowhere near our minds, and we actually were doing "pretty good." Yet both of us thought this would be a good idea. Hmmm . . .

Man, the first session uncovered some areas in our marriage that could definitely improve. It was helpful. I noticed a few areas in which it was beneficial to us and could be for you as well. Here are five ways preventative marriage counseling can help your marriage:

1. *Become aware.* You may not know your marriage needs help. A conversation with a counselor may reveal you are further apart than one or both of you realize. You may think your marriage is an eight while your spouse thinks it is a three. That can't last for long as it means somebody's needs are not being met.

2. *Talk about what you haven't talked about.* Sometimes your daily routine of work, kids, and everything else keeps you from talking about certain things in your marriage. Perhaps one spouse was afraid a blowup was inevitable if a certain touchy topic was brought up, or you just didn't get around to it because of life, but it was looming in your minds. Maybe it's "not the right time." Well, when you have a counseling session, it is always the right time.

3. *Stay accountable.* Great counselors give you some action items. After all, if you go to counseling, talk, and do nothing, it is useless. If you don't take action on these things, you will have your counselors in addition to your spouse to answer to.

4. *Gain some marriage wisdom.* Remember Proverbs 15:22 says, "Plans fail when there is no counsel." You don't know everything about marriage. Learning from the experience and mistakes of other couples can help you prevent, or grow through, your own challenges.

5. *Show good intentions.* If you go to marriage counseling, no matter how your marriage is, you are seeking improvement. We went because we had been married long enough and witnessed enough divorces close to us to know that the small challenges, which seem insignificant, can become way more than they appear. That is something we don't want. And we understood someone else could help us recognize and address these areas.

Here are some questions to help you while wearing the Wedding RING:

1. What are some challenges you anticipate in marriage?
2. How do you expect to grow in your faith as well as your marriage through those challenges?

Chapter Six

Ring #3—DiscoveRING

"Marriage is our last best chance to grow up."
–Joseph Barth

T hey say the most learning that happens in our lives happens from birth to age five. During that time we are little sponges soaking up anything and everything, both good and bad.

I'd say that is true for the most part. That is until you get married. Once you get married, it's like being a toddler all over again. You will learn a lot. You'll learn a lot about your spouse and a lot about yourself.

And if you are honest with yourself, you won't like everything you learn. I learned the slow, methodical pace my wife always seemed to have doesn't bode well when you are trying to be somewhere on time.

And she learned the way I had a place for everything and kept things so organized and that was rooted in some tendencies that weren't always attractive to her. In fact, they could be downright annoying.

This part of your marriage is the equivalent of having the covers pulled off of you, or worse, having the shower curtain pulled back with you behind it. Once you commit, say "I do," and are together more than you've ever been, you will discover things. A lot of things.

This can be the beginning of the end for many couples. For others it can be the beginning and crucial part of a lasting and fulfilling marriage. You absolutely have to wear the DisoveRING if you are to experience the full amazingness of marriage.

If you "have" to wear it, then you might as well embrace it and get prepared for what will take place when it happens. Wearing the DiscoveRING will do at least three things in your marriage.

1. *It will make you second-guess your decision.* You will see, hear, and even smell things from your spouse that you could not have imagined would ever come from them.

2. *It will make you feel like marrying him or her was the best decision you have ever made.* Have you ever had one of those moments when your spouse did something and you got caught up? Ladies, you saw your man at his manliest ever, and it did something to you; or you saw him at his weakest point, and you felt closer to him than ever. Guys, you saw a strong, yet tender side of your wife that you didn't know existed. Or you saw her wake up in the morning with no makeup on and her hair undone, yet she looked as beautiful as ever to you.

3. *It will make you realize you are not so hot yourself.* Out of all the things you discover about your spouse that get on your nerves, you'll realize that you have just as many flaws as your spouse, if not more. It's humbling and so good for your relationship if you embrace these discoveries.

Discovering things about your spouse is one of the greatest gifts you have in marriage. I love it when I "discover" something about my wife I never knew before. As we grow together in marriage, I feel I am continually pulling back layer after layer to reveal my wife at a deeper level.

I admit sometimes what I learn is frustrating and leaves me feeling like "wow, this is a problem," but it ultimately leads me to a deeper appreciation of her.

Emotional Roller Coaster

One of the pitfalls of the DiscoveRING is allowing those things that get under your skin, or reveal the flaws that are in your spouse, to dictate how you relate to her. It's going to happen. He is going to do or say something that reveals a really nasty character flaw, or maybe even an issue that just so happens to be a pet peeve of yours.

To many couples this is the first real challenge they face. One of the biggest ones for me was how quickly and seemingly easy, to me, my wife would break down crying. I couldn't believe it. On one hand I felt like her emotions and the tears that followed would fluctuate as the wind blew. East wind, she's happy. West wind, and the water works would flow.

On the other hand, I felt like I had done something wrong. When she would break down crying, she wouldn't want to talk. She would completely close up. So at first I thought, *What's going on?* Then when I finally got over my shock and frustration that she was all-out crying when nothing had happened and tried to comfort her, she closed me out. Which would lead me to believe I was the problem.

I felt like I was on this emotional roller coaster. And I don't even like roller coasters!

It was rough on both of us. I have to be honest, at times it is still hard to deal with for both of us. There was a time when it happened and I would close up. It was my version of throwing in the towel or throwing my hands up and chalking it up as "here she goes again" and "I can't do anything about it, so why bother."

Over time I realized how hard it was for her. While I was complaining internally and playing the victim, she was hurting not just from what was causing her to cry but also from her inability to control it. She'd try so hard not to cry, then finally it'd bubble over and she couldn't hold it in any longer. The more I asked, "What's wrong?" or "How can I help?" or "Why are you crying?" (with an attitude), the more it increased her emotion.

I learned the problem wasn't always with me. We both discovered that her tender heart was by design. God wired her that way (see Ps. 139:13–14), and it was for a purpose. My wife has this gift where she can feel the pain and even the joy others have and be right there with them. Our first marriage mentors once told her in a counseling session we had to never change that. God has purpose in it.

And we've found that to be true. She has a discernment that leads her to pray and intercede for others in ways I can only imagine. I'm just the opposite and almost harsh or cold at times. If something doesn't bother me, I don't always see or understand why someone could be so bothered by it. She literally feels it, sometimes physically, and will take those feelings to God in prayer.

Because of this people find it easy to connect with her on an intimate level that makes them feel comfortable and at ease with her. And she has been a blessing to many people through the prayers she's prayed as a result of her tender heart for others.

Now it is something I appreciate and something that makes me love her even more. Something we discovered early that was a major point of contention is now something totally different. It is still hard on her, but she understands it and knows there is purpose in it now. Had we discovered this frustrating thing and stopped there, we would have never experienced the good that could come from it. It could have actually been the discovery that led to the beginning of the end for us. Praise God it didn't.

The Goal of DiscoveRING

Now you can see why discovering things about our spouses and ourselves is so important. It will bring you closer together, or it will push you further apart. Your response to what you discover will dictate the effect it has on your marriage.

I didn't always choose to respond in a beneficial way. I learned the hard way. From my own stubbornness and stupid mistakes. I'm hoping by reading our story you can learn from some of those mistakes. I'm hoping by reading our story you will embrace good and bad discoveries in your marriage, with an understanding they can all have purpose. And remember, we are all growing. Some of those bad habits I had back then, I have grown out of them or intentionally made changes for the better. But those changes didn't come from my wife looking at me like I was crazy, nagging me, or walking out on me. They came from a desire to be a better husband and have a better marriage covered with a lot of God's grace.

Some habits and issues you have may never go away, but that doesn't mean your marriage doesn't work, you have irreconcilable differences, or it's time for you to find greener grass. It just may mean you need to grow. A pastor once told us in a counseling session that we are like a chisel and rock, and God is the hammer. Sometimes I'm the chisel and other times she is. God uses either one of us at different times to help mold the other into the shape He wants us to be. Don't get mad at your chisel, and don't be too hard on the rock. Something wonderful is being created through it all.

I once made a public confession that I would no longer be "notoriously bad" when it came to birthdays, Christmas, anniversaries, and holidays. Especially when it comes to my wife's birthday.

I said, "From this point forward I'm going to be notoriously great," in this area. Well, on my wife's "23rd" birthday last year, before the day barely got started, I walked into the room to see her with tears streaming down her face! She spent most of the morning crying. My initial thoughts were, *You have got to be kidding me! I can't . . . I can't win in this area.*

Unlike in the past, this year I'd taken the initiative to plan in advance, set aside funds, and arrange care for our kids, but it didn't matter . . . tears were the result. And I didn't know what to do.

The What

Finally I picked myself up enough to go see what was wrong and how I could help. I didn't say much at first. Just put my hand on the small of her back and embraced her. Then she said, "Thank you."

What? Thank you? As you can imagine, by this time I am completely confused. I'm thinking, *What did I do?*

The surprise gathering I arranged the previous night didn't pan out as many of the couples I invited had schedule conflicts, so I made adjustments on the fly. I hadn't given her the gift I got her yet, and I don't even think she realized I got her a gift at this point.

Yet she says, "Thank you."

I finally say, "For what?" Her response . . .

"For making my birthday so special."

Really? Those tears were tears of joy? The tears weren't because the surprise gathering didn't work out as planned? Or because I arranged for our kids to be out of town, not realizing she had never been apart from our kids on her birthday, and a complete meltdown ensued as they were leaving? Or because it appeared I had not gotten her a gift?

Nope. Tears of joy because to her, she felt special on her birthday. Sadly it was one of the few times I've heard that from her due to my "notorious badness."

At that point I was still confused, but I was cool with it. If it's special to her, even though I was missing something, it was best just to let it ride.

The Why

Later on I discovered the deeper source of the tears, not without more confusion of course. The tears started because of a text message she received from our daughter. I read it and it said . . .

"Happy Birthday Mommy!"

By now you should know what I'm about to say. Yep, I was confused again. "Happy Birthday Mommy!" brought her to tears.

To give you some background info, our daughter was out of town alone (without us or our parents) for the first time ever. She had a weekend event with her Cru teen ministry group. She had recently got her first cell phone, and right before our eyes we were entering a new season with her.

And this all just so happened to be on my wife's birthday weekend. The text made her so emotional because our daughter rarely calls her "Mommy." Apparently that was too much for her to handle emotionally at the time. So the tears flowed.

As I processed it all, I learned something about me and about our relationship. Fellas, this can help you too. Sometimes our wives' tears and other emotions are not always what we think.

The Problem

My problem was I was more focused on me than on her. I wanted a certain response to what she was experiencing on her birthday. When it didn't happen the way I thought it should, it caused problems with me. Not with her but with me.

The longer I thought, the longer I festered, and the longer I had an emotional pity party about it, the more bothered I became. Almost to the point of doing or saying something stupid. Been there, fellas?

I've learned when your wife cries or does something else you don't understand, don't project your feelings or thoughts onto her.

Make it about her. Seek to understand what she is going through, with a clear mind and zero preconceived notions. Had I done that, half of my morning wouldn't have been wasted wallowing in a muck of "I'm still bad at this" or "there is no way I can satisfy this woman!"

Instead I'd have spent the time enjoying her, celebrating her, and letting her know how special she really is. That may have resulted in more tears, but I would have known they were tears of joy.

Ladies, this works both ways. Maybe your man is the silent type. Maybe that's his way of processing the world around him. Maybe you desperately want him to open up and think you're somehow the reason he doesn't talk more. If your husband is doing something you don't understand, don't project your own feelings on him. Seek to understand.

When you project your feelings and thoughts on him, you rob yourself of the joy of understanding your man better. It's much easier to perceive things the way you would process it and respond in a given situation, but not as effective. I'm not going to act like it's easy, but over time you can begin to appreciate him more, and he can appreciate you more for being proactive in understanding each other.

Your goal through experiencing the DiscoveRING is to come out on the other side each time with a better appreciation, deeper connection, and better love for your spouse. If you can do this, your marriage will be fulfilling. If you aren't able to do this, you may have ongoing problems as you will have new discoveries continually throughout your marriage.

Responding to Discovery

As I mentioned earlier, your response to the new things you learn about each other will dictate where your marriage goes from there. So, how should you respond? There are several ways you can respond which will help you make it through this ring while continuing your progression to subsequent rings of marriage.

Acceptance and Love

The first and most important thing is to accept and love them for who they are. All of their flawed self. After all, haven't you been accepted and loved in the same way? God has accepted you and all your flaws, and He loves you like nobody else does.

So, no, your spouse is not perfect. Yes, he has a pretty nasty habit of not putting down the toilet seat or cleaning up around it when he misses. It's ridiculous that he leaves food crumbs all around where he ate. Or that she leaves a mound of hair in the sink after she combs her hair in the bathroom. When you can accept them and love them like that, you can easily accept them and love them at their best.

Remember Your Commitment

Okay, you get it now. Or did you forget?

"To have and to hold, from this day forward, for better, for *worse* . . ."

My friend Mark Merrill says this can happen in marriage, "What was once appealing is now annoying."[1]

You committed to loving them when they are appealing *and* annoying. When you discover these things about them that aren't so appealing, don't lose sight of your commitment. Stay committed to your commitment.

Don't Try to Change Them

Perhaps your spouse would be a better person if he or she just changed that habit or behavior. Perhaps your spouse knows it's something he or she should stop doing or should be doing, but aren't. It doesn't matter. It doesn't do you or your spouse any good for you to focus your efforts on changing them.

Frustration will be the result. For you and your spouse. The only person you can control in this entire world is yourself. Start there. Instead of trying to change your spouse, work on yourself. And during the process you may see them change as well.

Appreciate Their Differences

It's one thing to accept them as they are. But it's even better to appreciate them when they do things differently from you. This was one of my biggest issues in the early years of our marriage. I thought if things weren't done the way I thought best, then they were done wrong. I didn't appreciate the fact that my wife was different from me, and brought different experiences and different ideas into our marriage.

My wife likes surprises while I like to know up front so I can plan. My wife takes her time, I mean really takes her time. I seem to be in a hurry most of the time. We are different in many ways, and after years of banging my head on the table over this, I can now truly appreciate these differences.

You Are Flawed, Too

It's so much easier to point out someone else's sin and neglect our own. Or to recognize our sin but give ourselves a "pass" while holding another person, your spouse, to a higher level when it comes to their issues. Don't do it. Everything you learned about him or her that seems crazy, just take a minute and think about the craziness they discovered in you. You know you better than anybody else. You know you have some crazy in you. Don't forget it. You are flawed, too.

Pray about It

You can't sweep it under the rug. There is no rug big enough to cover it up. But maybe you feel it's impossible to talk to them without one of you blowing up or becoming offended in a major way.

"What is impossible with men is possible with God" (Luke 18:27). If you are worried about how a conversation may change your marriage, don't worry about anything; instead pray about everything (see Phil. 4:6).

I've learned the more I pray, and the more we pray together, the more connected and transparent we're able to be with each other. We are able to talk about potentially volatile stuff, we are able to talk about our insecurities, we are able to talk about anything. We can be completely transparent. Discovering something annoying about yourself can be handled much better when it's covered in prayer.

Find Out How You Can Help

What I found out is many of the things that bother me about my wife bother her just as much, if not more. It's the same with me. Before it bothers my wife, it has probably already frustrated me more than she knows.

Sometimes it's a skill or lack of skill type thing. There are some things we've been trying to change for years without success, but our spouses are gifted in this area.

Instead of using that as a tool to hurt them or show them up, see how you can help them. But they have to be willing to accept your help. If they don't want your help, provide support, be empathetic, find out what you can do, and do the best you can.

Discovering new things about you and your spouse can be great if you choose to make it great. It doesn't happen by accident; you must have some intention behind it.

Winning the Arguments

Once you are in the full swing of discovering new things about your spouse, the two of you are bound to have some disagreements. When it comes to disagreements in your marriage, you should have one goal and one goal only: to win! Yes, after the dust settles, you should be able to feel like "this was a clear victory."

I'm sure somebody has told you something different. That your chalking up a "W" at the end of a disagreement with your spouse is not what your intent should be. After listening to our marriage mentors teach us about solving disagreements, I now have a different opinion. One of the first things that changed my perspective was defining what a win was when it comes to disagreements.

If you and your spouse disagree on how to do something, then you have a discussion (or argument), and if the result is you do it how you suggested, then you win, right? No, winning the disagreement has nothing to do with whose way, or point of view, comes out on top.

Winning a disagreement in marriage has to do with coming out on the other side with both people feeling better about themselves and the marriage. Winning means resolving the conflict so that both of you feel loved and appreciated. Remember, this is the goal of discovering—to always come out on the other side with a better appreciation, deeper connection, and better love for your spouse. The same rule applies for disagreements.

I've never been a fan of conflict, and I admit I have tried my best to avoid or ignore it. But I've come to realize a lot of good can result from conflict . . . if it is handled in a healthy way. This happens when three things are present in the disagreement. First, both husband and wife *embrace the differences* that led to the disagreement. Then, they *learn from their differences,* and finally they *celebrate the differences.* Embrace, learn, and celebrate.

Embrace Your Differences

When you and your spouse embrace each other's differences, you create a safe place. The biggest challenge to conflict resolution is when one person (or both) doesn't listen. In order to embrace your spouse's differences, you have to listen to them.

Most people avoid conflict altogether because they don't feel safe. They feel their view will not be respected, considered, or even heard at all. Embrace the fact that you and your spouse are different, and you will sometimes (many times) have different opinions.

Learn from Your Differences

I began playing basketball when I was about three years old and went on to play in college. I have played on a lot of teams, and on all of them I noticed almost every player had a different skill set. They had different strengths, different places they liked the ball, and even different areas where they struggled. Knowing these differences and how they complement each other led to winning games and championships.

The same occurs in marriage as we have differences with our spouses. If you embrace them and learn from them, you can better understand how they can help you grow and grow your marriage. You'll truly be winning in marriage when you do this.

Celebrate Your Differences

I've known my wife more than half of my life. And I've told her many times that I am still learning new things about her. New things that intrigue me and make me love her even more. When you experience those WOW moments with your spouse, even after knowing her for more than twenty years, it's an amazing thing.

That is the product of embracing your differences and learning from your differences. You discover new stuff, and new stuff is worth celebrating because it helps you grow as a couple.

You can now win EVERY disagreement in marriage.

That is the blueprint for winning. You know if you won because of how you both feel after its over.

If you feel loved and appreciated, you got that "W." If either is absent, think back and see if both of you embraced, learned from, and celebrated your differences. Then proceed to winning in marriage!

Do You Know Your Spouse?

I was asked the following questions as a prompt for a series of blog posts I was writing.

Do you know your spouse?

I mean, do you REALLY know your spouse?

They made me think deeply about how well I *really* knew my spouse. As I thought about what I would write in response to those questions, I realized that I desired to, and should, know her better.

Does it ever feel like you're living with a stranger in the house? My wife, of course, is not a *complete* stranger, but sometimes I realize how little I know about her. (The more you learn, the more you realize how much you don't know, huh?) I would love to be able to complete her sentences (although she may not like it . . . wait, she probably says I already do!). I would love to be able to know what she really wants and expects of me and not be dumbfounded. Is that even possible, husbands?

This led me to think of ways to get to really know my wife. What could I do, what can you do that will help us to really know our spouses?

I thought of some of the times when something about her was revealed that I didn't know, good or bad. The situations when I really learned the most about who she really is. These are the times that enable both you and me to really know our spouses. From those discoveries I've pulled together a few takeaways I hope will help you too. These are my top ten ways to help you *really* know your spouse.

1. *Read and discuss books (especially the Bible) together.* Read regularly and discuss what you read. Many times you will have a different perception or understanding of what you read. When you do, you'll begin to learn how he thinks and interprets the things around him.

2. *Do something new together.* Find an activity that neither of you have much experience with. Take tennis lessons, karate, golf, salsa dancing, Chicago-style stepping, rock climbing, swimming, something. Just make sure both of you are newbies and can learn it together. You will be out of your comfort zones and probably looking a little silly, but your spouse is there looking silly at the same time. Witnessing your spouse when she is being stretched will teach you a lot about her.

3. *Ask questions and really listen.* I think most people ask the question, "How was your day?" But how many times do we really listen to the answer? If we're not careful, that can become almost a greeting and not really a question for which you care to receive an answer. So ask the question and really listen when your spouse responds. Take it deeper and ask more engaging questions about what they've said. You may have to gauge the amount of questions you can ask, but no matter the number of questions, focus on really listening. You can learn a lot by listening to your spouse.

4. *Take notes.* In school you take notes. In job training you take notes. In church some take notes. When it comes to your spouse, take notes. Study your spouse and record your

findings. Yes, study your spouse like a test, like a book, like a skill you're developing, and write it down! I recently began doing this, and I record it in Evernote. I record gift ideas, likes/dislikes, sizes, insights, favorites, pics of keepsakes, etc. Your spouse is way more important than a test or training class and is worth the time to take notes.

5. *Date them regularly.* Spending regular one-on-one time is something I cannot emphasize enough. When my wife and I are consistent with date night, I feel really connected to my wife. I feel like I do know what she wants and expects of me and what she wants to say next. Besides getting to know your spouse better, it is just fun to hang out. We'll spend more time talking about date night later in this chapter and in subsequent chapters.

6. *Play games.* You will learn a lot about your spouse doing this! I found out just how competitive my wife actually is (she will cheat to win), and she found out that I will deny ever getting beaten by her when or if I do! The true character of your spouse will definitely come out! *Haha.* It is also good to play games against other couples. You'll learn how your spouse performs when pressured and how he handles ups and downs.

7. *Pray together.* I've said it before, but praying together is one of the most intimate times you can spend with your spouse. When you are in God's presence, there is no hiding. Real concerns, real challenges, and real thankfulness will come out. You can learn what your wife thinks about herself and sometimes about you too. But that is okay because you really want to know your spouse. And you want to be transparent enough that she knows you.

8. *Spend many, many years together.* About half of marriages end in divorce, and many others are still legally married but separated. If you really want to know your spouse, spend

years and years together. That is the single best way to get to know somebody. Spend a lot of time with them.

9. *Go through something together. (This is inevitable.)* We have gone through job loss, homelessness, and living with friends/family, being broke, family health issues, multiple disagreements, legal issues in business, etc. You name it and we have probably experienced it. When you get in situations like that, character is revealed. Sometimes it is not what we want or like to see, but it does help you to know your spouse better. The key is to go through it together. If you are in one corner and your spouse is in the other, then you won't learn much. But together you'll learn a lot!

10. *Discuss and make plans to achieve your life goals.* Find out what is really important to your spouse. What is he really passionate about? Then begin to plan together how you will achieve or obtain that. Knowing what is deep down inside and working with him to get it will bring you closer and give you a greater understanding of what moves him.

If you really want to know your spouse, then begin to do some, if not all, of the things I listed. Knowing your spouse really well should be a goal of every married person. When married couples do that, then seeds for healthy marriages are planted and ready to harvest.

Don't Neglect Dating

One of the biggest mistakes we all make in marriage is we stop doing the things that led to our getting married in the first place. We stop opening doors for our wives, she stops wearing that dress or outfit her husband loves so much. Instead of keeping a car so clean she could put her makeup on in the reflection, she doesn't want to touch the car.

After you say, "I do," is not the time to change up the program. It's time to be consistent, it's time to go deeper, and it's time to do even more of what led here.

One of the biggest things many couples neglect after marriage is dating. They fell in love on a date or dates. Dating is what led you to getting married, and dating is what will keep you married.

We fell victim to this in the worst way. I suggest couples date weekly, but it's okay to miss a weekly date every once in a while. No matter what your dating frequency preference is, make it regular and consistent. We consistently didn't date and missed more than just a few here and there. We missed a lot.

We didn't just miss a week, or a month, or a quarter, or even a year. We missed years, plural. There was a period of time where we didn't date at all. We didn't even consider it. We had no idea we were even missing date nights.

At first we didn't get it. We didn't realize the importance. We were caught up in life, in giving birth and raising kids, and trying to make a living. But later we understood the importance of dating in marriage and were big proponents of it. In word at least. We still didn't practice it. That is until the last couple of years when we've been consistent in dating. Weekly dates became our thing, and our marriage benefited because of it.

Dating in marriage consistently is one of the best ways to continue discovering new things about your spouse. Especially for those of us with children. Having children can significantly reduce the amount of meaningful adult conversation a couple can have. This conversation leads to connecting on a deeper level. Spending this consistent, meaningful time is what leads to remaining friends and becoming best friends. And remember, best friends equal best marriages.

Becoming Best Friends

Do you remember having a best friend as a kid? What was it like with your best friend? If you were like me and my best friend, you did just about everything together. In elementary school you played together at recess and probably sat at the same table for lunch. In middle school you rode bikes all around your neighborhood or maybe even all over town. In high school you knew whom you'd be hanging with when the weekend came.

It would be hard to find you without your best friend. You spent a lot of time together. Then you began dating, and the person you were dating was the one you spent a majority of your time with. The amount of time you spent with your boyfriend or girlfriend outweighed the time you spent with all your other relationships. This person was the equivalent of your childhood best friend.

You eventually married that person. But is that person you married your best friend today? A Google search returned the following result for the words *best friend*:

"The one friend who is closest to you."

These words should describe our spouses. Our spouses should be the friend that is closest to us. Sadly, this is not the case for all of us. For those whose spouses aren't the closest to you, it probably started the day you stopped dating or trying to learn more about your spouse. You fell victim to the lies that prevent you from dating. You can't find a sitter. You don't need to date your spouse when you see each other daily. You don't have money to go out all the time. You don't know what to do.

Don't stop dating and don't stop discovering. My wife and I had a great experience with this a couple of years ago when we attended a weekend marriage retreat. This had to be the most perfectly timed weekend away ever! We were at a point where we just needed a break. A break from work, a break from home, a break from kids, almost even a break from each other.

We were tired and worn out prior to the trip. We were ready to get out of all things normal to us at the time. Once we arrived, we just felt so much relief. We had a weekend alone without any responsibilities. I don't even think I took my laptop. Since work doesn't really stop for me, I usually keep my laptop with me on trips, even personal or family trips. But this weekend I decided it wasn't getting opened.

While we were at the retreat, we crossed a line in our marriage that had never been crossed before. Our best-friend status came out in a major way, a surprising way. At the time of this retreat, we had known each other for more than twenty years and had been married twelve years.

Yet both of us had something we'd never shared with each other until this particular weekend. We both shared a deep secret and personal challenge we had been facing. We were both shocked at what was revealed. And we were both hurt, but the feeling of complete honesty and transparency outweighed it all. We did what best friends do. We shared our deepest concerns, thoughts, and our hearts. After we shared, I felt like I knew my wife like never before, and she felt the same. If we hadn't achieved best-friend status before, we definitely did during that moment.

We had a desire to be best friends, but I'm not sure we truly were until that moment. We crossed boundaries, tore veils, and opened doors. Maybe you are in the same boat. Your desire is to be best friends with your spouse, but you can't seem to get there. Or maybe one of you feels the other is your best friend, but it's not mutual.

My friend and mentor, Dr. Clarence Shuler, has written a couple of books on being best friends with your spouse. Dr. Shuler and his wife were the keynote speakers for that particular retreat. We met them for the first time there. He has some great insights on what prevents us from being best friends with our spouse.

1. *You are selfish.* That best friend from back in that day, remember them? One reason they remained your best friend was because they were there when you needed them. It didn't matter what was going on, they showed up. At the time you had a need, your needs became more important than their needs. Sometimes in marriage we do just the opposite. We put our needs before our spouse's. We are selfish. It's what I call the "give me what I want, and I'll give you what you want" method in marriage. It always fails and will prevent you from becoming best friends.

2. *Fear and your past get in the way.* Past hurts are a major stumbling block in marriage. Past hurts can prevent the transparency needed to discover new things or allow new things to be discovered.

Holding onto past hurts will not allow you to become best friends. Think about your childhood best friend. Can you think of anything they didn't know about you? Few things probably come to mind. They knew your good and your bad; yet it didn't change how they felt about you or how they treated you. You felt safe with them, and you should with your spouse as well.

3. *You lack commitment.* You must give yourself fully to your marriage. What my wife and I shared with each other that weekend at the retreat said, "I'm all in." It said, "I am totally, unequivocally, and fully vested in our marriage and in you." What we shared could have easily blown up in our faces, but it didn't. Instead it showed how committed we were to our marriage. Her problem became my problem, and my problem became her problem. We both committed to help each other through it.

Becoming best friends with your spouse will help you now and as you experience the following rings. Especially the PerseveRING. This ring will test your best-friend status like no other experience will.

Making Date Night Fun

So you finally got a night away from the kids. It's just you and your spouse. An evening alone, an evening doing adult things, an evening where you can do and say what you want. You arrive at the restaurant, the hostess seats you, and . . . nothing. Another boring date night. Have you been there? Maybe you are there now?

With date nights like this, why even have them?

My wife and I understand the importance of date night. We do our best to make it consistent, to make it a staple in our relationship. But we've found ourselves in that situation before. Out on the town and bored.

One culprit was a lack of variety in our date nights. Dinner and a movie can get old. On other occasions we found our conversation to be limited to "family business," i.e., the kids and work. It was almost like we didn't know each other outside of the life we built around our kids and our work.

How can we keep date night fresh and fun?

In order to keep date night fresh and worth the hassle of getting babysitters, staying out past your bedtime, and putting on your "going out" clothes, something has got to change. But what can be done to change it? Perhaps some fresh date-night ideas at our disposal and a list of conversation starters to guide our dates to keep us from defaulting to kids and work talk.

To close out this chapter, I am giving you two lists I hope will help you grow by leaps and bounds in this DiscoveRING phase of your marriage. The first list has some great ideas for conversation starters to try out on all your upcoming date nights. The second list has some creative and fun date-night ideas to put your conversation-starter-ideas to use. Enjoy!

25 Date-Night Conversation Starters*

1. What is one area of communication that I am good at and one area I really need to work on?
2. What are the top three goals you want to accomplish in the next twelve months?
3. If money were not a factor, what would you choose to do the rest of your life?
4. One thing I really enjoy doing with you is _____. What is one thing you really enjoy doing with me?
5. If you could witness one historical event, what would it be?
6. What can we do as a couple to make a change in the world?
7. When have you felt most loved by me?

* Visit my website for a digital copy of this and additional resources.

8. What is your first memory of me?
9. What are your biggest fears?
10. How can we make our marriage "affair proof?"
11. If you could have one superpower, what would it be?
12. Do you think our marriage makes our kids or other couples desire to be married?
13. What would you say is your biggest strength? And mine?
14. What is your favorite food, color, book, Bible verse, hobby, song, movie, sitcom, season, etc.?
15. What is the best time we've had as a couple?
16. How can I encourage you more?
17. What is your favorite childhood memory?
18. What is the most important lesson you learned from your parents?
19. What is the most embarrassing thing you've ever done?
20. Do you prefer "this or that" for example: read or write, run or bike, camp or cruise, etc.?
21. What would you do with $1,000 or $1,000,000?
22. Describe the perfect marriage.
23. What actor or actress would play you in a movie about your life?
24. How can I pray for you?
25. What is one thing we can do today that will make us better tomorrow?

25 Fun Date-Night Ideas

1. Go tandem bike riding.
2. Train for an event.
3. Cook a meal together or take a cooking class.
4. Read Song of Solomon together and discuss.
5. Have a couples' game night.
6. Go go-cart racing.

7. Learn kickboxing.
8. Test drive expensive cars.
9. Sing karaoke at a local restaurant.
10. Order takeout and camp out with a tent in your backyard.
11. Play Twister . . . just the two of you.
12. Play dance or exercise video games.
13. Borrow or rent a musical instrument and create a song.
14. Volunteer at a local soup kitchen.
15. Create lunch bags and drive around looking for homeless people to bless.
16. Use your family membership for the zoo, museum, etc. . . . go without kids.
17. Attend movies in the park during the summer.
18. Take a long lunch and go to a daytime movie at the theater.
19. Visit open houses.
20. Take a walk.
21. Go to a professional or college sporting event.
22. Go to a drive-in movie.
23. Go to a corn maze or pumpkin patch.
24. Rent a room and act like you are out of town.
25. Build or repair something together.

Here are some questions to help you while wearing the DiscoveRING:

1. What did you or do you expect to learn about your spouse or yourself in the early part of marriage?
2. How did or how will this discovery refine you?

Chapter Seven

Ring #4—PerseveRING

*"More marriages might survive if the partners realized that
sometimes the better comes after the worse."*
—Doug Larsen

W e looked at each other and couldn't believe it had come to this. We were in the middle of a discussion about my wife going to stay with her mother, who lived an hour away in the town we grew up in. The kids would go with her as well.

We were both scared, but we didn't know how else to make it work. How did it come to this? We knew this would change the game drastically in our lives. Our kids would be forever impacted, and we both didn't think the impact would be good. Our relationship wasn't that bad, and we wanted to be together. But we were about to be homeless, and for some reason this was the "best" solution to the problem.

I needed to earn money for us to eat, eventually find a place we could afford, and get back on our feet. The income-producing opportunities were here, the city we were in, so I couldn't leave without missing out on opportunities to make money.

If Stephana went back home, she'd have a place to sleep, she'd have food, and the kids would be well taken care of. I'd just be in "grind mode" and do what I had to do to make something happen for us.

It seemed wise at the time, but it was not! That decision—that move—would be the beginning of the end of our relationship and our family. Facing the challenges we were facing alone would be a sure way to fall to them.

Fortunately, that move never happened. For whatever reason, whether we were too scared to do it or the fact my mother-in-law said it was not a good idea, we decided against it. We decided to fight the challenges we had together.

That decision followed a theme in our marriage since the beginning. According to some of our friends and acquaintances, we were always together. If you saw one of us alone, you were sure to see the other one nearby. We were always doing things together.

In church we served in many of the same ministries. We made trips together. We went to the store together. We attended our kids' events together. In hindsight this may have helped us make the decision not to separate while working through our financial problems. We had become used to being together, doing things together, and experiencing things together—good and bad.

In essence we had become one, and while we were experiencing pain and struggles, the potential pain and struggles of being apart were much greater.

Things got pretty uncomfortable shortly after that. We had to move from our home, and while we didn't have a home to call our own, being together made everywhere we stayed feel like home. Our living quarters may have been tight in some places, and our privacy may have been limited, but we were together. It was important and a crucial step for us to make it through this season in our marriage.

"It is not good for the man to be alone" (Gen. 2:18).

I don't want to imagine going through what we went through alone.

Beating the Odds

When I was in real estate, I remember some of the people we worked with saying, "They don't build homes like they used to." At one point new homes and new neighborhoods seemed to pop up overnight. The homes and subdivisions all looked great, but what many of our contractors discovered was they weren't built as well as homes built years ago.

The homes seemed to break down and have issues that older homes took years to develop. Well, today the same can be said of marriages: "They don't make marriages like they used to."

Statistics reveal disturbing information that say about half of marriages end in divorce and most within the first few years. That's disturbing for a couple planning to be married or for a couple young in their marriage.

But what can you do? How can you prevent your marriage from ending up on the wrong side of the divorce statistics?

My wife and I made it through those years, although we almost didn't make it through the first year. We've had some serious challenges that would end most marriages. We've survived job loss and financial strain. We've made it through homelessness twice! We've dealt with in-law challenges. And we've survived parenting!

If you are second-guessing getting married or you're in a marriage you don't think is going to last, don't give up. Have hope and be encouraged. If we made it, you can too.

I want to share some insight about what has helped us and other couples persevere and beat the statistics. Here are five ways to divorce-proof your marriage.

1. *Just say no!* I've said it before, and I stand by it. Not allowing the word, thought, or anything related to divorce in our marriage put us in a place where we had no choice but to make our marriage work. We burned all bridges by agreeing never to consider divorce or even speak about it in our relationship. No matter how hard it got, we chose to "just say no." It's a choice you may have to make over

and over again, but it's a game-changing choice that can save your marriage.

2. *Ignore the statistics.* The stats say you have a 50-50 chance of your marriage making it. To me stats are numbers on a paper, not real people. Instead of focusing on those numbers, talk to real marriages with real stories of what works in marriage. We learned from the marriages that seemed to be working and working well. I encourage you to do the same. Find marriages that have good qualities you like and learn how to implement those traits and habits in your marriage.

3. *Pour a lasting foundation.* Just like houses, the foundation of your marriage is important. If you build your marriage on something that is shaky, you can believe your marriage will be, at best, shaky. Marriages built on shaky foundations will eventually fall down. We chose to build our relationship on biblical principles for marriage. The principles in the Bible are lasting. When your marriage is based on them and you truly live out those principles, your marriage will be lasting too.

4. *Make marriage a priority.* I love sports and especially the game of basketball. Marriage didn't change that, but if I spent too much time with basketball and my friends who love basketball, then my marriage would feel it. And it wouldn't feel good. Making marriage a priority means making it the number-one relationship, except for your relationship with God. Date nights are needed. Trips together and time alone are musts. Your marriage must become more important than work, ministry, and even your relationship with your kids.

5. *Nurture your marriage.* My wife is a great nurturer. When our kids were born, she was able to nurture them in ways I could not. Without her nurturing, our kids' growth and development would have been hindered. The same goes for your marriage. You have to treat it like a baby by nurturing it and feeding it.

We read books, we take classes on marriage, and we attend weekend retreats. We've also had marriage counseling on multiple occasions and joined couples small groups. All of these things have helped to grow and improve our marriage. Without this nurturing our marriage's growth and development would be hindered.

An amazing marriage is yours for the taking. Your marriage can beat the statistics. You can have a fulfilling, lasting, and complete marriage. You can divorce-proof your marriage. Adopting the five ways above will help you do so. I encourage you to try them in your marriage.

Pushing Buttons

I've been married almost fifteen years, but my wife still pushes my buttons sometimes. And I know I still push hers. This week was no exception. I'll be honest, this was the first day this week we've really had some decent conversation. Most of the silence was predicated by me.

I've come to understand there will be times like this in marriage. It is reality in any relationship. Books and poems have been written about it, and of course songs recorded. One of my favorite music artists is Christian Rap artist Lecrae, and his song "Buttons" practically became my theme song this week. Yes, the frustration was high. I had to rely on a theme song to keep it together.

Although I've listened to "Buttons" many times, a few of the lyrics jumped out at me this week. I'm certain it was because of the friction between Stephana and myself. Below are some of the lyrics and a look into my life this week.

> For better or for worse
> Sometimes I make you sick, and you get on my nerves
> Make it work
> I ain't goin' nowhere, and I give you my word
> I will be right here
> So though you push my buttons
> I ain't leavin'
> You can keep on pushin'
> I ain't leavin'[1]

I could not have said it better! Although I made her sick, she made me sick, and we got on each other's nerves, neither one of us was leaving! We might have been sitting up in the same room, mad, not talking, and laying blame on the other (in our minds), but when it all boiled over, we were going to keep on pushing.

So, what do you do when your spouse pushes your buttons? Lecrae gave us a blueprint of what you can do.

1. *Remember your promise.* When we got married, we made a promise to each other and, most important, to God. From time to time we need to reflect on that, especially in tough times.
2. *Understand there will be issues, but work through them.* If anyone told you marriage is happily ever after all the time, do the opposite of any advice that person gives you. Marriage comes with challenges, but anything that is worth having is worth overcoming the challenges!
3. *Be there.* Whether you are mad or not, be there. Even when I was out working all day, or Stephana was running around with the kids all day, we both knew when we came home the other was going to be there. No questions asked.
4. *Accept your spouse as he or she is.* We all married flawed people. Sometimes those flaws really push us, but don't let them become the focus of your marriage. Accept your spouse as he or she is, even when your spouse is pushing your buttons. Stay with them and love them even more.

If you have been married longer than a week, then you have probably been at this point before or are currently there now. I encourage you to do as I did: listen to the wise words my man Lecrae spoke in "Buttons," and apply them in your marriage.

The Blame Game

In boxing they say the punch that knocks you out is the punch you don't see. Throughout a boxing match both fighters throw and receive multiple punches. I believe about 99.9 percent of those punches would knock me clean out, but for the most part, they are able to withstand them. Every once in a while a boxer gets hit with a punch he didn't expect or didn't see coming. The result is usually devastating, many times resulting in a knockdown or even a knockout.

Our relationships are similar in the fact that we are faced with many challenges, and for the most part we are able to withstand them. One thing in marriage is similar to the knockout blow a boxer didn't see coming. It can come in a flurry of other issues and never be seen. The result can be a broken relationship or one that never becomes truly fulfilling.

What is this threat to your relationship? When we are caught off guard, it eats away at our relationship from the inside before finally destroying it. We have to avoid it at all costs.

What is it? It is blame.

Blaming your spouse destroys the foundation of a healthy marriage. It tears down your spouse and makes him or her the enemy. It kills trust and intimacy by making your spouse feel alienated or like she is playing on the opposing team, which puts her on the defensive.

What do you do about this threat?

If the blame game is being played in your relationship, it is something that must be cut out. But you first have to recognize when the blame game is being played.

Here are three ways to recognize the blame game is present, so you can avoid it.

1. *You use superlatives when describing something bad that happened.* My wife calls me out for my use of superlatives all the time. I *always* seem to be using them.

"You always."

"I never."

"Every single time."

I'm guilty as charged! If you notice you or your spouse using superlatives to describe negative situations, then you're playing the blame game. Pay attention to your language, and choose different words to describe the situation.

2. *You overuse, "if, then."* An "if, then" statement means whatever happened after "then" is a result of the "if."

"If you hadn't, then . . ."

Perhaps something your spouse did was the cause of something negative. However, other factors may be at play that are not always obvious. Instead of jumping right to "if you . . . , then . . . ," begin to consider the big picture.

3. *You are reactive.* As I've mentioned before, one of my favorite books is *The 7 Habits of Highly Effective People* by Stephen Covey. One of the habits is being proactive, which means you view situations based on what you can do before they actually happen.

It's the opposite of being reactive and basing your view on what others did or didn't do or could have done. When we find ourselves being reactive and not being proactive, we are playing the blame game.

I encourage you to become aware of when blame is present in your relationship and begin to eliminate it. Knock out blame before it knocks out your relationship.

It's the biggest threat to your relationship, especially when you are unaware and it creeps in, catching you off guard. Protect your marriage from being knocked out by hitting the blame game first.

Fault Lines

You have probably experienced storms in your marriage. Most marriages can withstand a storm or two every now and then. Marriage storms can typically be predicted, just like real weather-related storms can. And you can usually tell how long they will last.

While some storms can come and go quickly, and many times predictably, other marriage issues may seem to come out of nowhere. Similar to an earthquake, this thing seems to come when least expected, catching anybody in its wake off guard. But do they really? Do your major, destructive problems come out of nowhere? Or have you been unaware of the existing fault lines?

Fault lines are not playing the blame game. I am not talking about whose "fault" it is, so you can put down that finger you have pointed at your spouse. So, what exactly is a fault line? The definition of the word is literally:

"A divisive issue or difference of opinion that is likely to have serious consequences."[2]

A fault line is something that will divide you and lead to some serious mess in your marriage. Physical fault lines are located beneath the surface of the earth. So they are not easily noticed. The only way a fault line can be recognized is by going deep. By looking below the surface.

Is your marriage surface-level, or do you go deep?

To go deep in marriage, open and honest communication is needed. To go deep in marriage, you must go through something and stay together. To go deep in marriage, a commitment in good and bad times is needed.

If your communication is weak. If everything is "perfect." If your commitment has not been tested. Then you may have a surface-level marriage.

Fault lines can eventually cause a marriage "earthquake." A physical earthquake is caused by an abrupt fault-line shift. Almost immediately the earthquake releases "built-up stress" that has accumulated over time. Rewind . . . *"releases built-up stress that has accumulated over time."* . . . It is probably safe to say I am in somebody's kitchen right now.

But wait, there is more. Take a look at what else an earthquake is. It is something that is "severely disruptive" or an "upheaval."[3]

Basically it is something that turns your world upside down. To the point of destruction. Wow! Can a marriage survive something like that? Only if your marriage is prepared and you know what to do.

By going a little deeper in your relationship, you can uncover some potential fault lines. Here are several to be aware of:

- Loose lips or gossip
- Lack of trust
- Laziness (spiritually)
- Pornography
- Overspending
- Foreclosure
- Unwillingness to work
- Sickness
- Substance abuse
- Flirting
- Blended family relations
- Relocation
- Putting anything or anyone (but God) before your spouse

- Lack of respect
- Unmet expectations
- Unequally yoked
- Job loss or loss of income
- Infidelity
- Little white lies
- Minimum communication
- Death of parent/child
- In-law relations
- Lack of support
- Not taking care of yourself
- Lack of quality time

How to Survive a Marriage Earthquake

The Los Angeles Fire Department (LAFD) is pretty experienced in dealing with earthquakes. Their method of surviving physical earthquakes is great for surviving marriage earthquakes as well. According to the LAFD you can do three things to protect yourself during an earthquake.

First, DROP down to your knees *before* the earthquake knocks you down. I can't help but see the image of a couple dropping to their knees in prayer. Go to God the minute you feel a shake. Many couples go to others for advice first. Mistake. Go to the Author of marriage as your first layer of protection.

Second, COVER your head and your entire body if possible. Protect what is in your head, your thoughts. If you continue to feed your mind negative thoughts about your marriage or your spouse, then you are opening yourself up to something that could permanently damage your marriage. The same with your body, do no let anything unwholesome taint your body.

Third, HOLD ON until the shaking stops. A marriage earthquake is the time to hold on tighter to your spouse and to your commitment. He needs you more than ever, and you need him more than ever. The shaking will stop eventually. So don't let go prematurely. When the shaking is over, you can pick up the pieces knowing you have survived something that destroys many other marriages.

PerseveRING Marriage Storms

Storms in your marriage are inevitable. Just like thunderstorms, you know at some point there will be one. Thanks to weather forecasters, we are usually forewarned. But what about storms in our marriages? Is it possible to know in advance when they are coming, or are we just at their mercy? More important, how do we prepare for the storms?

I'm willing to bet you own an umbrella, probably a raincoat, and, if you live in one of the northern states, snow boots and gloves. It would not be the smartest thing for you to disregard purchasing those items. You may not need them every day, but when a storm comes, you are glad you have them! I wonder how many of us take precautions for the storms in marriage.

We prepare for almost everything in life. In just about every area of our lives, we prepare for the worst-case scenario. We are advised to save for a rainy day. As mentioned earlier, we purchase items and prepare for various types of weather. Most of these things we prepare for are not things we necessarily want to face. Yet we know we will. So, why not do that in marriage?

A meteorologist has tools that let him know what type of weather to expect. The financial planner does too (your bank statement). Even life insurance underwriters have information that can give them a good idea of your life expectancy. If all those things can be predicted, then we should be able to predict the storms in our marriage. Right?

How to Know When Storms Are Near

I think it is completely possible to know when a potential marital storm is near. Just look at yourself. Look at what consistent actions you have taken (or not taken). If you have spent more money than you make, expect a financial storm. If you have taken more than you have put into your marriage, you may be nearing a storm.

Here are five warning signs a marriage storm is near:

1. *You have not spoken your spouse's love language.* If you don't even know what his love language is, or what the five love languages are, go get your umbrella.
2. *You have not been truthful.* All relationships are built on trust. If you have broken that trust, or said something that could, then get ready, a storm is brewing.
3. *Communication is lacking.* We are built to relate to others. We are left unfulfilled when we don't. When the communication is lacking in your relationship, you should not be surprised if issues arise when you do start talking.
4. *You are not praying together.* I do not see how any marriage can thrive, let alone survive, without God involved. However, many times couples only go to God alone, not together. This is an area that many times goes unnoticed. At least until the storm.

5. *You have an island marriage.* An island marriage is where you become isolated and do not allow other married couples that have been there, are there, or are going there to get involved. When doing so, your minor problems seem major, and the storm is getting closer.

Preparing for Storms

The best way to prepare for the storms in your marriage is to expect them and know they will pass. If you think marriage truly is happily ever after all the time, then the storms that hit you while you are unprepared are the ones that could knock your marriage out. Here are some additional ways to prepare:

1. *Have your storm gear ready.* Bible verses about God's plan for marriage, babysitters to watch the kids in case of emergency, an advance agreement that no storm will end in divorce, or even entertaining the idea of divorce!
2. *Know that storms are not always going to be there.* If you think the storm is the norm, then you are in some trouble. Understand this too shall pass.
3. *Have a storm crew.* Some storms you cannot fight alone. You need a crew of trusted couples, counselors, and family members you can go to and they will speak truth to you.
4. *Create your weather as best you can.* Yes, storms will come. However, if you know your actions (or inactions) are the perfect weather pattern for a storm, then make some changes.

Go through storm survival training. Periodically, you should prepare your marriage for tough times. Things like regular dating, attending retreats, having weekend getaways, or meeting with a small group can help. Those times will build your marriage strength to help you withstand the storms.

⚜

This past weekend we were at my teen daughter's basketball awards banquet. She's homeschooled, and all the girls on her team are homeschooled. Because it's a homeschooled team, they have no home gymnasium, no home court to play their games, and the girls come from all over the place to be part of this team.

The team is really good, and they made it to nationals and placed sixth in the nation for homeschooled girls' basketball teams. As the coach spoke about the girls and some of the girls spoke about their experience playing, a common theme arose for me. Hard work. The coach mentioned how hard the girls worked. The girls mentioned how rewarding that hard work was.

I didn't notice one girl say she wished it wasn't hard, nor did I hear any of them complain about it. These teenage girls all embraced the hard work that it took to be successful on their team. One girl not only worked hard on the court but drove over an hour for each practice and worked two jobs so she could afford the travel and cost associated with it.

If these teenage girls understand that becoming successful, and experiencing the great things they experienced, requires hard work, then why do grown folks complain and let it deter them when they hear marriage is hard work? That amazes me. It is widely accepted and expected that hard work is required to achieve good things in life, except when it comes to marriage.

Blood, Sweat, and Tears

Marriage is hard work, and that's a good thing. When it comes to marriage, there is not a problem with the words *hard work* being included in the same sentence. You can't expect to get through this PerseveRING successfully without some real work. The name says it all! I'm thankful marriage is hard work. From a man's perspective, when a woman is "easy," we don't want to marry her.

So I want to encourage you to not let the phrase "marriage is hard work" scare you. Appreciate the work you put in to make your marriage great, realizing that nothing good in life comes without some type of work. This includes marriage.

Blood, sweat, and tears in marriage? You better believe it! Marriage is the most wonderful thing in the world, but don't be confused. There will be bloodshed, you will get sweaty, and both the wife *and* the husband will get all teary eyed. If that seems harsh, don't worry, that is what makes marriage work.

I am willing to say if you have not bled, sweat, or cried then your marriage may not be the best it could possibly be. While we try our best to avoid them all, they are coming, but so are the greatest days of your marriage.

Sacrifice (Blood)

Before you go there, do not worry, nobody is getting cut! Bleeding in your marriage is about sacrifice. The union of two people from two different households, with two different upbringings, means sacrifice is a must. One definition of *sacrifice* is "the offering up of something precious for a cause or a reason."[4]

Your marriage is bigger than you, so sometimes you have to "take one for the team." Until this happens in marriage, needs will go unmet. A marriage with unmet needs is one that may not last. But a marriage where sacrifice is how you roll will be filled with two selfless individuals meeting needs and growing together.

Work (Sweat)

Did the word *hot* come to mind when you read that subhead? Well, it is the first thing that came to my mind. I pictured me running, working out, or just being outside on a hot, humid day. Most of us have heard that great marriages take work. Sometimes you have to get down, dirty, and sweaty.

Marriage can act like a physical trainer. You will be pushed to points no human being has ever pushed you to. You will do things you never thought you could do. When you do, you will sweat; sometimes you will sweat profusely! Those of you who work out know when you reach that point you can expect great results. There is no playing cool in marriage; go ahead and put in work.

Release (Tears)

Tears in our bodies serve multiple purposes. The types of tears we are most familiar with are emotional tears. Those tears come when we've experienced some emotional high or low. But think about how you feel before those tears come compared to after they are released. You feel good after.

Sometimes you just need a good cry. The tears in your marriage allow you not to hold on to things. It may hurt, but you are not intended to hold on to it. Let those tears flow, and release the emotion that triggered them. This frees you up, allows you to think clearer, and allows you to move to a place of healing in your marriage.

PerseveRING through Family Issues

Family issues happen to everyone. Sometimes we bring them on ourselves. Other times they happen through no fault of our own. Family issues are part of family life.

I can recall a particularly challenging week for our family. We experienced a waterline break in our neighborhood causing us to temporarily be without water. This happened to be on the worst morning possible for our family. Later that day we had to take our three-year-old to the ER due to coughing and breathing complications. This led to him being admitted to the hospital for a day and a half.

It was a rough stretch, but I knew we'd get through. If you have family issues of any kind—big ones, little ones, and all in between—be encouraged. You, too, will get through. Thankfully, Scripture provides us with wonderful promises to hold on to when our family is up against the toughest issues. Here are seven promises that are key in helping to persevere:

1. You are unbeatable because God is always with you (Josh. 1:5)!
2. Things are working together, and good results will come from them (Rom. 8:28).
3. Despite the way life may look, you are a winner (Rom. 8:37)!
4. God wants to help you, and He will if you ask Him (Ps. 55:22; 1 Pet. 5:7).
5. Even in tough times, good things are happening (Ps. 112:4).
6. God's grace is enough, and His power is strongest when we are weakest (2 Cor. 12:9).
7. The challenges you face now pale in comparison to the blessings you'll receive (Rom. 8:18).

The promises God made in these verses encourage me, and they can do the same for you. Read them, ask God what they mean and how they apply in your family life, and refer to them frequently. Whatever you are going through, you will get through it. I am rooting for you!

Parent Meetings

Let's get practical. We've talked about weathering the big storms. I've shared promises from Scripture you can cling to when the bottom seems to fall out beneath you. But what if you're just trying to make it through the day? Have you ever gone in your bedroom with your spouse, locked the door behind you, and ignored your kids? My wife and I have, and we plan to do it more often. In fact, we believe doing so consistently is going to improve our marriage.

We got this idea from some friends of ours, who do this daily. They call it a "parent meeting." While it seems like a desperate move to get away from the madness of your kids, it's not. It's actually an intentional way of spending quality time together in your marriage, uninterrupted by your kids.

Our lives are filled with stuff every day. Work stuff, ministry stuff, and of course our kids' stuff. For us, since having three kids, much of the stuff that fills our lives is their stuff. While the marriage relationship should be the priority, it seems to take a back seat for many families.

When we aren't careful, there are stretches of time where my wife and I are only alone when we are asleep in bed. That is not healthy . . . not healthy at all. So we have to be intentional, and a daily parent meeting is a brilliant way to have time alone consistently.

How Does It Work?

We are a home-centered family. I work from home, my wife works and schools our kids from home, and of course we live in our home. So, when I "leave" for work, I go through our garage, through the laundry room, and into my little office. It's less than a ten-second commute. And my office door is never locked so I get "visitors" from time to time.

In the past our parent meetings have only happened after we've spent a long day together as a family and we come home. My wife and I go to our bedroom, close and lock the door (as our four-year-old rarely knocks), and we spend time together. The kids are instructed not to bother mommy and daddy unless there is an emergency (somebody is bleeding and they can't stop it, or a limb is missing).

Consistency Is Key

The only problem with that is it didn't happen daily. We typically did that on the days we met with our homeschooling group, as that is a long day for us. But after I had a conversation with another dad about it (he calls it "couch time"), I realized it has to be done more often . . . daily.

Parent meetings are now held every single day when I "return" from work. This provides many benefits. First, we have that time alone five days per week. In addition, I have to shut my working day down consistently at a certain time. I have to set up some boundaries and honor them.

Every Marriage Needs Parent Meetings

Whether the quality time in your marriage is lacking or not, you have to use the parent meeting in your household. It'll add more quality time to a relationship where it's not an issue. And it'll fill the void of quality time for those relationships where it's nonexistent.

Here are some benefits daily parent meetings will provide in your relationship:

1. *Takes out the guesswork.* Not sure when you'll have a moment just to relax with your spouse, when you're not both dead tired? Daily parent meetings take out the guesswork. You will get that moment every day. That is a game changer.

2. *Gives you both time to unload.* Did something special happen, or something that frustrated you? Parent meetings give you the opportunity to share that special thing, or that thing that got under your skin.

3. *Helps you stay connected.* We both work from home, and sometimes we have no idea what's going on in each other's lives. That fifteen or thirty minutes per day helps you stay connected. A weekly or monthly parent meeting doesn't provide enough time to share all that is happening, unless you are having smaller daily meetings.

4. *Guarantees time for you to be intimate.* I don't know how you roll, but the parent meeting might be your time to . . . to do that. To some wives that may be the last thing on your mind at that time, but believe me, it's not the last thing on your husband's mind.

5. *Teaches your kids that your marriage comes first.* Having a marriage-centered family is important to us. Many marriages end after the kids leave home because the kids came first; it was a kid-centered family. When your kids see you daily spending time together, they'll get it, and they'll respect your relationship. Your family will be strengthened by this.

Having daily parent meetings is a must. Maybe you call it "couch time" or "mommy-daddy time" or "kid-free time." It doesn't matter what you call it or how you present it to your kids. Just do it, and watch the dynamics of your marriage and family change.

Unmet Expectations

Sometimes our marriage storms are caused by external factors. Sometimes they are caused by our own mistakes. Sometimes they occur because we just don't know what to expect or we haven't communicated our expectations clearly enough to our spouse. Every one of us came into marriage with certain expectations. And every one of us has dealt with the disappointment of unmet expectations in marriage. It is one of those things in marriage that will happen. When it does, it can make you or break you.

A year or so ago my wife and I were asked to be a part of a group of seven couples all looking to grow our marriages. The group was led by a couple that has been married over thirty years. All of the other couples have a similar family makeup. Most have been married seven to twelve years, have young children ages three to thirteen, and are thirty-somethings.

The couple leading the group views this group as their way of paying it forward. By their sharing the ups and downs of their thirty-year marriage, they are equipping another generation of marriages to be successful. (By the way, this is what the MentoRING is all about.) My wife and I are thankful for the group and for this couple.

One weekend we discussed the topic of unmet expectations in marriage.

What happens when marriage expectations go unmet?

As I mentioned earlier, all marriages will be met with some level of unmet expectations. It is what happens after this that determines how it affects your marriage. Your natural reaction may begin at disappointment. The disappointment may turn to hurt. After the hurt comes anger. Once you get angry, you turn that anger toward your spouse in the form of punishment. In other words, you make your spouse pay for not meeting your expectations.

Unfortunately these stages happen without us being aware. It is hard to change something you are unaware of. Well, now you know. So, what should you do about it?

There is a better way to deal with unmet expectations. You can be sure if the above pattern is followed in your marriage, it will be a rocky marriage at best. However, once you make yourself aware, you can be intentional about changing that pattern and learn to persevere.

You can better deal with the unmet expectations and even grow your marriage through them. I encourage you to put into practice the following four ways to deal with unmet expectations, and watch your marriage change for the better.

1. *Love and forgive your spouse.* When you exchanged marriage vows, you committed before God and your spouse that you would stay committed through everything. Honor this commitment, in spite of your spouse's failures and his falling short of expectations. The need for forgiveness will never go away in your marriage, so get good at it!

2. *Communicate with the intent of understanding your spouse.* Many times when expectations go unmet in our marriage, the other person wasn't even aware of what was expected. The only way to know what is expected is to talk about it. Make regular communication a part of your marriage. Don't make knowing your spouse's expectations a guessing game; talk about them.

3. *Change your perspective.* In the real world of marriage, you will never be able to meet all of your spouse's needs, and she will never be able to meet all of yours. We were never intended to do so. Some needs can only be met by God. Develop this perspective and allow your spouse some grace in some areas.

4. *Don't throw your expectations out the window.* Some expectations may be unrealistic and unfair to your spouse. That doesn't mean to lose hope in them or your spouse. Part of your marriage

purpose is to help each other grow. Continue to strive toward your hopes and aspirations. Work toward them, pray about them, and do it all together.

Here are some questions to help you while wearing the PerseveRING:

1. Name three benefits of persevering through a difficult situation.
2. Name a time when you personally had to persevere through something difficult.

Chapter Eight

Ring #5—RestoRING

*"The number-one thing a man wants for his family
is to keep his family together."*
–Pastor Eric Wiggins

W hat happens when you realize you are in a dead marriage?
Is it time to throw in the towel, or is it possible to bring life
back to your marriage? A dead marriage, or one without love, is a
real problem for many, including at times my own marriage.

The question so many couples ask is: "How do we get our marriage to be *in love* again, like it used to be before we were married?"

After fourteen years of marriage, my wife and I have experienced
many seasons in marriage, and not all of the seasons were enjoyable.
The divorce statistics show "falling out of love" is common, as about
half of marriages end in divorce. It's a scary place to be, and it can
seem like it came out of nowhere.

The reality is, if you've reached the point where you feel like you
are no longer "in love," or your marriage is dead, it's been happening
over time. It's just like how people who are in over their heads in debt
didn't accrue that amount of debt overnight. The debt was created by

one financial decision after another that finally reached the point of overwhelming them.

There is good news. Just as a series of choices can lead to massive debt, or a dead season in marriage, a series of choices can lead you out. We will kick off this chapter with five things you can focus on to bring life to your marriage and fall in love all over again with your spouse.

1. *Rebuild your foundation.* You may or may not have started with a good foundation to your marriage during the Engagement Ring. If you did but you've drifted, you need to revisit that. Think about the guiding principles in your life and your relationship. If you've never set a solid foundation, it's never too late.

No foundation is built without first having an idea of what the final result will be. When you said, "I do," what did you envision for your marriage?

And more important, why did you envision those things? Let that be your start, and begin to discuss what you can do daily, weekly, monthly, and yearly to achieve that. Don't be afraid to put the Engagement RING on again and work on that foundation.

2. *Go to school and "major" in your spouse.* One statement that seems to go with "we are no longer in love" is "I don't know my wife anymore." Which makes sense because for you and me to love a person, or even a thing, we need to have some sort of intimate connection or knowledge of them.

I've mentioned my love for basketball. I started playing basketball at around age three. I played competitively since the third grade all the way through college and even play in adult leagues now. I've spent a lot of time getting to know the game of basketball, and because of it I fell in love and remain in love with it to this day.

If we are to remain in love with our wives, and vice versa, we need to intimately know them. We need to discover things about them and never stop trying to discover new things. We've already talked about the importance of having regular date nights. What a great way to restore the love in your relationship! Dating is how you fell in love before marriage, and dating will be how you stay in love after marriage.

3. *Draw a line in the sand.* Let's be completely real. Marriage is NO JOKE! Two people with two different upbringings and two different personalities and two different life experiences coming together as one? There is nothing easy about that.

A time will come where you feel stuck, and a time may come where you want out altogether. This is where you draw a line in the sand and not just once but every single time any of those feelings come up.

Your line in the sand says we will not entertain anything except making our marriage work. No matter what challenges we face, we will persevere and restore—not walk away. And that means not just staying together but being fulfilled together. This means there is no separation, no divorce, and no mention of it at all. It won't be easy, but it's possible. You just have to decide.

4. *Put things back in place.* I don't know what you've faced in your marriage. There may be things broken, feelings hurt, and things done which you feel you can never come back from. Don't believe it. Your marriage can be restored; the pieces can be put back together.

This involves consistently doing the three things mentioned before. But it also includes going the extra step or mile. It means loving your husband unconditionally by not dwelling or "beating him up" over minor things. It includes speaking to your wife in a way that makes her feel loved and speaking her love language.

And most important, it includes putting your marriage in the proper place and making it a priority. The relationship with our kids is not number one; our marriage is.

When you make your marriage a priority, it gives life to your marriage.

5. *Appreciate and enjoy your marriage.* I heard a quote that said, "You take your spouse for granted until you are walking by the casket." That's extreme, but it's real. My wife and I have seen

the unexpected loss of a spouse firsthand when my sister lost her husband to cancer and when a close friend died of cancer, leaving behind our friend/her husband.

While our marriages are not only about our enjoyment, they are meant to be enjoyed. Our marriages can and should prosper. Your marriage can prosper, but it gets to the point of prospering by your taking one small action at a time over the course of your marriage.

I encourage you to take the actions that will restore and give life versus take life from your marriage.

Restoring Friendship in Your Marriage

I know plenty of stories of married couples that were together but were not friends at all. Sadly I must say I can relate. There have been times in my marriage where we weren't really friends. We were more like business partners; our kids were like our employees or customers. They were the people we focused on pleasing. This put our relationship and our friendship at a distant second, or worse.

It's not a good feeling. The thing is, you don't always realize it. It kind of creeps up on you. It's like the silent relationship killer. It is silent but deadly. Your relationship will not survive if you are not friends. Well, you can remain together, but your relationship will not be truly fulfilling.

The question is, what do you do when you realize you are married but not friends? Maybe you were before, but the friendship seems to have dissolved. Can anything be done? Yes, but things may not change overnight. Just as your friendship didn't deteriorate overnight, it will not be restored overnight. But if you begin to take steps today, then it will be restored sooner rather than later.

Here are five ways you can restore the friendship in your marriage:

1. *Go back to basics.* At some point you were friends, and during that time you talked to each other differently, you treated

each other differently, and you showed a different level of respect. Somehow through the ups, downs, and experiences in your relationship, you began to take things for granted. You stopped doing the basic things that made you fall in love. Basic things like opening car doors for her, cooking meals for him, making special trips on the way home before meeting each other, dressing in your best, or putting on that special cologne or perfume they liked. Get back to the basics that made you fall in love in the first place.

2. *Stop saying yes to everybody else.* One of our biggest challenges was commitments for our kids, commitments for ministry, and of course, work. Some things you have no choice, but with others you do. Stop saying yes to everybody else, and say yes to your spouse. Instead of filling your schedule up with all these things, leave space for you and your spouse. You say yes to your spouse by saying no to these extra nonessential things.

3. *Get desperate about date nights.* If you've done point 2, then you've made it easier to make this happen. When you free up that time, block it out for you two to be together. I wrote before about how we were desperate for date nights. We had to make some changes, get out of our comfort zone, and just not let anything stop us from having date nights. Dating is how you grew your friendship. Dating will be how you restore your friendship in marriage.

4. *Talk, talk, and talk some more.* Communication is the key. It will unlock the possibilities in your marriage. Communication is how friendships are made. Do you have any friendships where you don't communicate? Maybe you have some friends you don't talk as much with anymore, but at one point there was a lot of communication, which is the reason you are able to "pick up where you left off" each time you talk. This goes for your marriage. Talk about silly stuff, talk about serious stuff, and talk about your true feelings and

dreams. The point is to talk on a daily basis. If you haven't already, now is the time to put those daily parent meetings into place.

5. *Prioritize your friendship.* One of the biggest barriers to friendship in marriage is making other relationships a priority over your marriage. Marriage is the number-one relationship you should have with another person. This includes your relationship with your kids. Some people don't like it, but putting your kids, your parents, your girlfriends or buddies ahead of your spouse will keep your friendship from developing to it's highest level, which will keep your marriage from getting there.

RestoRING the Spark

The first step in RestoRING the friendship in marriage is to get back to basics. The point of going back to basics is to jump-start the restoration process of a stale relationship. A good way to do this is to reminisce on your early dating days. The days when you were courting and trying to determine if she was the one. Sometimes when life hits and you experience a lot in your relationship, you forget. You forget what attracted you to each other, and you might even forget how you both looked back then if your bodies have gone through some changes.

There was something he used to say that he no longer says. There is something she did that she no longer does. The longer you are in a relationship, the easier it is to function like a business relationship. It takes intention not to be so . . . boring. The staleness or boredom comes when the emotion of your relationship is missing.

Continually reminiscing can spark those flames again and restore anything that seems to be missing from your relationship. Here are a few ideas to help you reminisce on your early dating days:

1. *Go to the place you had your first date.* This is sure to bring back some special memories. What were your thoughts on that first date? What did he say or do that stood out to you? Talk about those things, and relive the moment.
2. *Hang out together where you used to hang out back in the day.* My wife and I went dancing a lot. We don't do this today, but we can reminisce, laugh, and watch the people doing what we used to do.
3. *Catch up with some old friends who knew you when you were dating.* Who are the people who knew you back then? They know some things not everybody knows about one or both of you. Catch up with them and talk about it. There are sure to be some good memories, and maybe even some you wish didn't happen. It'll make you appreciate being with each other today.
4. *Visit the spot of your proposal.* The restaurant where I proposed is still there but under a different name, and it looks totally different now. But it is still special to us both. I can remember what we were both wearing that evening. In fact, it is probably still in our closets. (We are parents of three . . . our wardrobe is number ninety-nine on the list of priorities!) Thinking of that always sparks something for us.
5. *Watch movies and listen to music from your dating days.* Thank goodness for Spotify and Pandora. Every so often we'll go to my nineties playlist and listen to the music we used to drive to, we used to dance to, and we used to . . . we used to really enjoy. . . . Music and movies will take you back quickly!

If you need to restart that fire, bring those good emotions back and restore what was lost in your marriage by taking a trip down memory lane. Regardless, it is fun and something different you can do with your spouse.

Turning Things Around

One of the most wonderful things about being married is the fact you have someone with you and for you at all times. It is a reciprocal relationship. Sometimes you need encouragement. Sometimes you need to encourage your spouse. I needed encouragement earlier this week, and my wife was there when I needed her.

The start to my week was rough. After a busy weekend, I was done Monday morning. Monday didn't care, as it had a ton of stuff waiting for me to do. I really wanted to climb back in bed and sleep all day. I just couldn't get going like I needed to. Fortunately, I am married to a wonderful woman. She stepped right in.

The wonderful part is, I didn't even have to ask her. She instinctively sprang into action and did her part to encourage me. As the day closed, and I had gotten out of my funk, I praised her and reflected on all she had done.

Although these actions were specific to our situation that day, some takeaways and common things can be used in your marriage as well. Without a doubt a time will come for you to encourage your spouse. Encouragement is an amazing way to turn things around in your marriage—your attitude, your perspective, your day, or maybe a whole season of life. When the time comes, these action items can help you quickly encourage your spouse.

1. *Seek first to understand.* I am certain my wife was just as drained as I was that day. Her weekend was just as busy, if not more so. She could have easily pointed out the fact I was slacking, as I was. She could have not cared how I was feeling, nagged, and condemned my actions (or lack of). However, she was patient, kind, loving, and understanding.

2. *Pray for and with your spouse.* I began to feel overwhelmed with all I needed to do. It was turning into frustration and sulking. I could see my day was not going to be productive, and some major ball dropping was about to happen. In the midst of this, she calmly

knelt next to me, laid hands on me, and prayed. It was just what I needed at just the right time.

3. *Speak your spouse's love language.* My love language is acts of service. She knows this, and she began to speak it. I had meetings, writing assignments, calls to make, a desperately needed haircut appointment I was trying to squeeze in, and a ton of other stuff to do. She filled every gap there was. She selected and ironed my clothes. Fixed a meal to get me started. Quickly got the boys ready so I could make it on time to my barber appointment. She even stopped what she was doing to come pick the boys up from our barber appointment so I could leave to attend a meeting. And she prepared the things I needed for my meeting.

4. *Take a backseat.* Keep in mind she had a ton of stuff to do as well. She probably had seven hours of sleep Friday night, Saturday night, and Sunday night combined! Her Monday morning duties didn't care about her weekend either. However, she put my needs before her needs. She put my needs ahead of her own. Next she put the kids' needs above her own. She willingly put her needs in the backseat so our needs could be met.

5. *Remind them of the big picture.* Even with her help my day was still full and challenging. I had to grind it out. That grind could have sapped me and had me right back in a discouraged state. However, she subtly reminded me of the big picture. She reminded me of why I do what I do and what is ahead. Her favorite Scripture, Galatians 6:9, summarizes this so well:

> So we must not get tired of doing good, for we will reap at
> the proper time if we don't give up.

I want to encourage you to take action when you see your spouse in need of encouragement. Taking the above five actions can quickly turn your spouse's day or mood around. He will love and appreciate your doing so. When you both consistently take these actions, your marriage will be better off.

RestoRING Prayer in Your Marriage

Have you ever had access to something that would help you, but you didn't use it? Or had the knowledge to do something but didn't put that knowledge to use?

Let me be the first to raise my hand!

Why don't we always do what we know works?

There is one thing I've talked about several times throughout our journey so far that I know works in marriage and has game-changing results. I believe in it and think it's great, but I haven't always done it. I've heard talks, sermons, attended seminars, and read books completely dedicated to this very thing, but for some reason I still don't do it enough. Sometimes it's completely missing from our relationship. Is it missing from yours?

But at some point I started to take action. I decided to just do it. And do it on a daily basis. It was a GAME CHANGER for my marriage. And it is so simple. Most days it takes less than five minutes to actually do.

I don't have to go anywhere, I don't need anything, and I don't even have to prepare for it.

All I have to do is grab my wife's hand, kneel beside her, or lie with her, open my mouth . . . and pray. That's it, prayer. Prayer is the ultimate game changer in marriage! It is the single greatest (and easiest) thing that can restore whatever is broken in your relationship.

As I wrote earlier, my wife and I have not always been faithful in praying, at least not together. Every single night we pray with and for our kids. Every single day we pray alone, if even a quick prayer. But we realized our prayer life together, as a couple, was almost nonexistent.

We attended a marriage retreat recently, and we were given a challenge. Actually, the husbands in attendance were given a challenge. The challenge was to work out every day alone and with our wives. Not physically but spiritually.

We were challenged to have a regimen of Scripture reading and praying alone before everyone in the house woke up. And then to follow that up with reading a psalm with our wives and praying together immediately after. We had to do this for twenty-one straight days, and our wives could not remind us if we failed to do so.

I accepted the challenge. Did I go twenty-one for twenty-one? Nope, not at all. But I made good on my promise more days than not. And after we reached Psalm 21, we didn't stop. We kept going. And our marriage is much better for it.

It's a simple thing for a couple to pray together. But I've learned that not many couples actually do it. Most of us have heard it, but we're not all doing it. James 1:22 (NIV) warns us, "Do not merely listen to the word, and so deceive yourselves. Do what it says."

But since we've done what it says, the game has changed in our marriage.

Praying together builds a stronger connection with your spouse. We pray in the morning together, and it helps us to better stay connected all day. Prior to that we found ourselves going about our own business each day as we started it in different ways and at different times. Praying together daily connects us for those moments together and guides our thoughts, words, and actions throughout each day.

Praying together builds better communication. Our communication with each other and God has grown. Going before God together breaks down all barriers. It gives you a look inside your spouse's heart and allows you a platform to discuss those tough topics in your marriage. It's amazing how the communication gap is now smaller since inviting Him into the conversation.

Praying together builds deeper intimacy. As the communication barriers are broken, you become more intimate. Intimacy involves sharing something with someone else that you don't share with everybody. Nothing is deeper than praying as one to God. The pastor at the retreat suggested praying together before intimate moments. We have done that, and let's just say I'm glad I listened and *did* what he said.

We knew prayer needed to be a major part of our marriage, but we were deceiving ourselves in this area. But since we began to actually do it consistently, my wife and I have experienced firsthand what God can do in a marriage filled with prayer.

I now issue the same challenge to you. Read a passage of Scripture and pray with your spouse for twenty-one days straight. Watch how God restores your marriage and family.

RestoRING Together

I know not every couple reading this book will be in a stage of marriage that includes children. But many are and most will be at some time. It's impossible to talk about RestoRING our marriages without bringing our children into the equation.

My wife and I were talking the other day about how loving our kids were to one another when we brought each new baby home from the hospital. Our daughter, now fourteen, just about loved her two little brothers to death.

Our oldest son couldn't keep the smile off his face and just couldn't get enough of his little bro. But sometimes today we can barely get them to stand next to each other for a photo, hug one another, or even be in the same room with one another without some type of disagreement or fight.

We should have expected this as we were warned. I can remember people telling us to enjoy it now but be ready for the time when all they do is fight. We kind of dismissed it, thinking, *Our kids won't be like that.*

While they do love one another, sometimes you can't tell, and sometimes our kids are "just like that"! As a parent it is tough to deal with, no matter how good we get at resolving disagreements. As men, we especially don't like it.

One rule of thumb that was true for me and most of my friends who grew up with siblings is, you are taught to stick together and to stick up for one another. If I were to get into a fight as a kid and my brother was able to help but didn't help, he'd be in hot water when we got home.

Or if someone was messing with one of us and the other allowed it to go on, that would not be taken lightly when we got home. I'm the same with our kids today. Our oldest kids know if someone is mistreating any one of them they better not allow it to go on. If little bro isn't allowed to play with the toys, the games, or anything else, then they know none of them should play.

It's almost a natural instinct type thing we instill in our family as men, and it hurts us to our core when it doesn't happen. And that doesn't matter if it happens when our kids are four and eight or when they are thirty-four and thirty-eight. That's because . . .

The number-one thing a man wants for his family is to keep his family together.

It is devastating for a man when his family is torn apart, especially if he could have done something to prevent it.

What I've come to realize over the years is living in the same household doesn't necessarily mean a family is together. It's not just a physical connection. It's an emotional, an intellectual, and a spiritual connection. When you're connecting with your spouse and kids on those levels, then you have a much better chance of keeping your family together, even when they have a choice to do otherwise. I want to share a few insights that have helped keep my own family together.

1. *We do more things together than apart.* When we first got married, I was still trying to hang with the fellas a lot. When I first made the decision to decline some of those times to hang with the fellas, it challenged some of my friendships. But it helped us grow closer during those early parts of marriage and building a family. Guys night out is not necessarily a bad thing, but when it comes before date night, or spending time with your family, then it is. People used to tell us they never saw my wife without me and me without my wife. We did a lot together, and it's paid off.

2. *We made church and other ministry activities a family thing.* Just about every Sunday you can find us at church. On Wednesday

evenings you can find our entire family at our kids' Awana Club. The act of worshipping together and developing spiritually is something that has been part of our family since shortly after our daughter was born. This simple practice of attending weekly services, plus Bible reading and praying at home, has been one of the most important staples for our family. We've all grown closer to one another because we've grown closer to God.

3. *We gather around our kitchen table daily.* I've said on my blog many times before that our kitchen table is the heartbeat of our family. It's where we eat, we meet, we do school, we pray, we launch businesses, we discuss our finances, and we talk. For many it is an uncommon thing to eat meals together . . . at home . . . at the kitchen table. For us it has been one of the major reasons our family has stayed together. When you have busy schedules and hectic lives, you have to have a place where you can come and slow down. Of course your house is this place, but even within our houses gadgets and all kinds of other stuff keep us apart. We've made our kitchen table just the opposite of that. It can be the same for your family.

We can't control everything that happens as our kids grow older and leave our homes, but we can have a meaningful influence on our kids and families by doing some simple things to keep our families together while they are still under our roof.

I encourage you to be intentional and give yourself a chance to have the number-one thing a man wants for his family . . . to keep his family together.

RestoRING Time

Two of my all-time favorite books are *EntreLeadership* by Dave Ramsey and Jon Acuff's book *Quitter.* Both discuss the topic of employees stealing from their company. As I read it and realized I have been one of those thieving employees, it was a nice gut punch. But even worse, an effective gut-punch combo, was the realization I've been stealing from my wife and kids just as much, if not more.

Employees steal in many obvious ways: taking merchandise, embezzling money, taking office supplies home for personal use. But the type of theft authors Ramsey and Acuff discuss isn't as easily recognized. In fact, many employees, including you, probably don't even recognize or acknowledge it as stealing.

I am talking about stealing time. When you agreed to work for your employer, they agreed to pay you for that work. That means during your work hours you are to be doing company work. Not Facebook, not paying your bills, not doing anything outside of the job you are paid to do. And you are to show up on time to do so and not leave early.

When you use this time for something other than this, you are stealing.

Stealing from Your Spouse

So if you can steal time from your employer, then you can definitely steal time from your wife and kids. If you are like me, you probably steal more time from your family than anything else. Being married with kids makes it easy to steal time from your spouse. You can find plenty of conspirators willing to help you. I have at least three that live with me.

Our marriage mentors have said, "Kids are an interruption in your marriage." That statement is so true. Their needs are your responsibility, and many times meeting those needs interrupts the time you are spending, or planning to spend, with your spouse. If you've ever been a "single couple" (married without kids), then you know exactly what I am talking about.

"PK," or prekids, you could come and go when you pleased. You could do what you and your spouse wanted to do. You could even do what you wanted, where you wanted, when you wanted, and if you decided to do it in your bedroom, you didn't even have to lock the door! Yes, sex is one of the "its" I am talking about but not the only "it." Date night was only limited by your imagination. Quiet time was not a problem. Of course "AK," after kids, things are different.

Stealing from Your Kids

Stealing from your spouse, "AK," is not the only problem. You are probably stealing from your kids as well. The biggest partner in crime to that is work. The very thing you do in the name of providing for your kids is the thing that steals one of your greatest gifts to them. Your time.

In my case I work from home about half the day and work at a school the other half. When I have not completed all the work I intended at home, it can feel like an interruption to stop and leave for the school. What do you think I do? I try to make up the time "lost" by taking it from my kids later. I effectively rob Peter (my kids) to pay Paul (my work). I come home and jump on the computer to "finish one more thing." I keep my face in my phone, reading e-mails, responding to messages, expanding upon ideas, or even just doing nothing to recover from my "long day." All the while my kids are missing their time.

Commit to Quit

Unfortunately you cannot return the time you've stolen from your wife and kids. You can't go back into last week, grab a ball, and go outside to throw it with your kids. You and your wife can't go to the Valentine's Day concert you missed earlier this year. It would be great if you could, but it's not happening.

What can happen is committing to doing away with your criminal ways, the stealing you do from your wife and kids. Picture yourself as a rehabilitated thief! No more stealing time from your family. Below are a few ways to get you on the road to recovery.

1. *Get up early in the morning.* Jon Acuff likes to call this "being selfish at 5:00 a.m."[1] Twenty-four hours sometimes just doesn't seem to be enough. Get more out of your day by waking early. You won't have to worry about stealing from your family because your family will be asleep!

2. *Determine nonnegotiable time blocks.* Block out some regular time intervals in your calendar for your family. Time for you and your wife, and time for you and your kids. Guard this time like Fort Knox. Don't negotiate, trade it, or do anything but spend that time with your family.

3. *Focus on one thing.* One of my issues is violating my own principles. I sometimes do not "do what needs to be done when it needs to be done." If you are working on Project A, Project A gets all your attention. If you are spending time with your family, your family gets all your attention. Multitasking is proven to be less effective than focused work.

4. *Be on time.* If you do the first three points consistently, you are on your way to making sure you are on time. When you arrive late, it steals from whatever you are late to, which makes it easier to steal from the next thing in line. My friend Kevin at SportsDadHub.com has a great suggestion to help this by being a time pessimist instead of a time optimist.[2]

5. *Don't be afraid to let some things go.* Some things are more important than others. And many days you will not be able to do everything you intended to do. That is okay. Prioritize the most important things; the less important things can wait if you don't get to them. Your wife and kids should always be at the top of that list.

Marriage Retreats

We're nearing the end of this chapter, and we've covered a lot of ground in regards to wearing the RestoRING. How are you feeling? Do you still feel like your marriage is stuck in neutral? Or for every step forward, you take two or three steps backwards? You are not alone. My wife and I have been there many times. One practical thing that always helps is a weekend away to attend a marriage retreat. We just talked about not stealing time away from your spouse. Here's a way to give back some of that intentional time!

Marriage retreats mean no kids, no work, no cooking and cleaning. Imagine that! I have to tell you, they are AMAZING! We get so caught up in the daily grind, we have no idea how much retreats are needed.

I am 100 percent convinced every married couple needs to attend a marriage retreat. And not just one marriage retreat but one every year. If you don't, your marriage may never be all that it can be. In fact, a marriage retreat may actually save your marriage.

During one particular retreat, the first thing we noticed was how long it had been since we had a weekend alone together. My wife confessed to me that she wasn't sure if being alone for so long would be awkward. That is sad; she wasn't sure if she could spend time alone with her husband of almost twelve years (at the time) without having weird feelings.

I wasn't sure what to expect, either. I most looked forward to just not having to do anything. It didn't even matter if we had sex or not. Yes, I thought that. As long as we ate, as long as I didn't have to concern myself with work and could sleep without kids waking us up, I was cool.

Once we got there, way late, things changed in a hurry. We were greeted warmly by the retreat committee, who graciously and patiently waited on us in our tardiness. We saw other couples milling about, we checked out the weekend agenda (seeing what we already missed), and were excited not only about the time away but to do something to bring us closer.

The first session we attended and the breakout sessions went to work on us immediately. Through the speakers' stories and marriage principles they shared, we began to talk like we never had before. Even sharing things we had never been able to share before. Instantly we were free, our guard was down, and there was no awkwardness. From then the weekend and our marriage kept getting better.

I wrote earlier about having a plan to improve your marriage. Make marriage retreats part of the plan. I encourage you to find a marriage retreat to attend this year. Your marriage will benefit in so many ways. If you're not convinced, here are my top five reasons you *have to* attend a marriage retreat:

1. *Take time away from "regular" life.* We all need time alone and time away from all that goes on in our lives. You do not want to get away so infrequently that you aren't sure if you'll feel weird doing so.

2. *Learn from someone who has been there.* We attended Committed for Life's Marriage Retreat, and the couple brought in to speak was amazing. At times I felt they were telling my story; yet they were providing sound principles on how to get through it and improve my marriage while doing so.

3. *Enjoy fellowship with other couples.* One of the greatest things was meeting other couples who were also working to improve their marriages. Couples in the same season; some in earlier or later seasons. It was encouraging and refreshing.

4. *Your marriage needs it more than you think.* Like us, you may realize your marriage isn't perfect but think it's okay. But when you go, you will realize your marriage can be so much greater. Plus you'll get help getting there.

5. *Show how much you love your spouse.* The ultimate reason for a marriage retreat is you love your spouse and are willing to do anything to show your love, grow closer, and have a better marriage.

No matter where you think your marriage is today, attending a marriage retreat should be a part of your marriage plan.

Unbreakable Marriages

Here we go. Some cold, hard truth to wrap up this chapter. I'm here to tell you—happily ever after is a myth! I have yet to experience or see a couple living happily ever after. But what I have experienced and seen is an unbreakable marriage.

I live in the Midwest where we have tornadoes. When a tornado touches down in the area, one way you know is by the broken trees it leaves in its path. States like Florida don't have tornados, but they have hurricanes. I'm not sure which is worse. But after a hurricane comes through, you don't see many broken trees like in the Midwest. Because they have palm trees. Palm trees bend but don't break. That is more like my marriage than happily ever after.

Both types of trees go through storms. One type of tree breaks; the other bends and bounces back when the storm passes. All marriages go through storms. Some marriages break while others bend and bounce back. What is the difference? What can you do to ensure that your marriage doesn't break but bends (perseveres) and bounces back (restores)?

A few habits can make the difference in a marriage that ends on the negative side of the statistics and an unbreakable marriage.

1. *The habit of communication.* Try to have a relationship, any type of relationship without communicating. It doesn't exist. Relationships are based on relating. Communication is a key form of relating.

2. *The habit of sex.* Sex is important. Sex is very important. Sex is the celebration of connecting in other ways in your relationship. Unbreakable marriages celebrate.

3. *The habit of spending time together.* I'm not saying a long-distance relationship will not work for a while. But if a marriage is to be unbreakable, then some quality time has to happen.

4. *The habit of laughing.* Laughter makes the heart grow fonder. Unbreakable marriages have fun, they laugh, they joke, and they have good times.

5. *The habit of praying.* Many marriages pray, but unbreakable marriages make it a habit. And they pray for and with each other. Try praying for your spouse when you are mad at your spouse. It works for unbreakable marriages.

6. *The habit of serving.* Serving is a selfless act. You cannot have an unbreakable marriage and be selfish. Unbreakable marriages make serving the other person a priority.

7. *The habit of commitment.* Commitment is not a one-time thing. When you are married, you have to commit continually. Year after year. Month after month. Day after day. Moment after moment. Doing so creates an unbreakable marriage.

Here are some questions to help you while wearing the RestoRING:

1. What is an example of something that's been restored and the end result is better than the prior?

2. How can this restoration apply in your marriage?

Chapter Nine

Ring #6—ProspeRING

"Some of the best times are tied to the hardest times."
–Dustin Reichmann

(W) hen we think back to the times we remember most, some sort of pain is often associated with it. Women who have given birth can probably relate to this better than men. Some of their greatest blessings, their children, came through great pain. Whether that pain was a few hours of labor, or carrying another baby, having excess weight, or anything else that comes with being pregnant for roughly three quarters of the year.

Our marriage is no different from that. I've mentioned some of the struggles we've had in our marriage and family, and those seem vivid in my mind. Yet we mention them in the same sentence with wonderful times in our marriage. Those times are inevitably hard.

It's deceptive to a degree and something that can cause a couple to mistake their marriage as not what it should be, or as unsuccessful. For the longest time we fell into that trap. Our finances, or lack thereof, have been our marriage's constant Achilles' heel. As a result we've occasionally viewed our marriage through the lenses of the state of our finances and found it to be lacking.

For you it may be your health or your fitness. Those of us with kids may view our marriage success in light of how well our kids are doing in school, or in sports, or just their overall (mis)behavior. None of that is your marriage as a whole. Yes, it makes up a part of your marriage, but it does not determine whether you are prospering in marriage or not.

In fact, I'd argue that the greater and more frequent your marital challenges are, the more ProspeRING you'll experience in marriage. At that point you are able—no, you are forced—to strip down all the extra stuff that gets in the way of your relationship, and your focus, appreciation, and dependence on your spouse become greater than ever before.

⚭

When Stephana and I spoke with Dustin and Bethany Reichmann, one of the biggest things Dustin said was the quote at the beginning of this chapter. Their best times were tied to their hard times.

They had difficulty answering the question about some of the greatest seasons in their marriage without mentioning a struggle that preceded or came with that great season. Both Dustin and Bethany began to list a series of challenging times.

- Frustrations from learning to live together when they were newlyweds
- The struggle of paying off debt
- The life-altering changes that came with each childbirth
- Career dissatisfaction and being unfulfilled, which led to a career change
- Launching their website, EngagedMarriage.com, which is now tied to their passions and callings in life

Dustin laughed because he couldn't mention a great time without a hard time. In that moment, he realized their fulfillment came from their growth together, sharing these experiences with each other, then sharing with others later. There is no joy without suffering. No compassion without struggle or pain.

There is not a ProspeRING without a PerseveRING and a RestoRING. So don't view the ProspeRING as an event or a destination. ProspeRING is growth through struggles that almost go unnoticed. Growing together, overcoming an obstacle, loving your spouse in spite of their shortcomings and sin—when you do this, you are experiencing the ProspeRING.

Lessons from Disney World

It's our family tradition to go to Disney World as the birthday celebration for each of our kids' fifth birthday. My wife loves Mickey Mouse but had never been to Disney, and we knew we wanted our kids to go. The advice we received was wait until they are at least five years old and then go. The thought process was, if you go before then, they won't be able to do or appreciate as much.

So we successfully went on the fifth birthday of our oldest child. Although the trip was an overall success, my wife didn't get as much enjoyment. She is the adventurer and physical risk taker of our relationship, so things that appeal to her are roller coasters, zip-lining, going super fast, and all things in between.

Well, if you do the math when it comes to the birth order of our kids and their years apart, you'll notice something. Our oldest is fourteen (at the time I'm writing this), our next child is nine, and our youngest is five. Child number one and child number two are five years apart. Which means at the fifth birthday of child number one, we either had a new baby in the stroller or a baby in the belly. It was the latter.

Stephana was close to eight months pregnant. Eight months pregnant at Disney in the summer! Let's just say she wasn't all that happy about being turned away ride after ride. She may or may not have been allowed to ride the Goofy roller coaster on the little kids' side.

So, out of all of us, Stephana couldn't wait the most for the next fifth birthday celebration to arrive. This was going to be different. And it was different in several ways.

The first Disney trip we made a road trip with my parents and my nephew, who was twelve years old at the time. We were also experiencing one of our most successful years in our business.

Disney trip number two was the opposite. I was at the tail end of a sales job in which my monthly sales and income had been steadily dropping over the past few months. In fact, one month after going to Disney, I lost my job because I was unable to meet my sales quota for multiple months in a row. Financially we were strapped.

So strapped that we actually ran out of money while we were at Disney World. Yes, we were away from home at the happiest place on earth, celebrating the life of our second child, and broke as a joke! We were only about halfway through our five-day stay when we noticed we had more days (and meals) left than money.

We had no clue how we were going to eat, let alone buy the kids any souvenirs. So we were forced to call our parents and ask them to send us money. How embarrassing and how stupid! I made the first call.

"Hey Dad."

"How is Disney, son? Is Jackson having the time of his life?"

"Yeah, he is. But . . ."

"What is it?"

"We have run out of money. We can probably afford one or two more meals before it's all out. Can you send us some money?"

My parents and my father-in-law sent us some money to bail us out. But even that came with difficulties. We decided not to rent a vehicle while in Disney to save money. We'd just ride the Disney shuttles and free transportation they provide within their properties.

To get the most of the money from my parents, whose money came first, I asked them to deposit it in our checking account. (We banked at the same bank.)

Well the closest bank or ATM wasn't close at all. I don't remember why we needed cash instead of using our debit card. My wife and I recently talked for about fifteen minutes about why we drove to the bank, but we couldn't remember. Whatever the reason it was not the best choice.

To get to the bank we had to leave Disney property and drive into the city of Orlando. We had no rental car, so we had to take a taxi. Keep in mind we were at Disney, one of the biggest tourist destinations in the world. We got our heads busted paying for that cab!

The cab ride there and back cost as much as a two-day rental car. An expensive two-day rental car. So a large piece of our money was spent just driving to get the money! We might as well have had them overnight cash to the hotel, wire the money for a fee, or just paid for the rental. At least we could have gone to the grocery, or anywhere else we wanted.

But we were thankful. We were at Disney on a budget, not just a "we have 'x' amount for souvenirs," but a "this is how much we can spend per meal, . . . and we'll have to share some meals."

That could have broken us and our marriage, but it didn't. We went on to have some of the best times of our lives. My wife got to ride roller coaster after roller coaster, which almost made the trip a success in itself. We got to eat, which made the kids extremely happy. And we just appreciated one another. This was experiencing the ProspeRING although we were in a broke situation.

All the "fluff" of Disney and all the extras were not options to us. But we had a roof (Disney property hotel), we had transportation (Disney shuttles), we had food (Disney cafeterias), we had tickets to each park, but most of all we had one another.

Our kids have no clue the struggle we had on that trip. My wife and I sure do. But we all know the fun, the good times, the memories, the Mickey Mouse-shaped waffles, and days swimming at the pool.

Had we not persevered through previous struggles, had we not discovered a thing or two about each other, had we not held on to the dreams we had together, and had we not established a foundation to live our lives and grow our marriage on top of, we may not have seen that Disney trip the same. But all that we'd experienced allowed us to truly have a ProspeRING experience in a situation that many other couples would have viewed as nothing of the sort.

When you realize the best times are tied to the hardest times, you will see and experience prospering in your marriage.

Tandem Bike Riding

There is a lesson in everything! And there were plenty when my wife and I joined some of our friends for a "fun" outing. This "fun" outing was riding tandem bikes at our downtown canal. All I have to say is, if you are currently enjoying the ProspeRING season of marriage, try something new and "out there" like tandem bike riding. You'll learn a lot and find out how strong your marriage really is!

Tandem biking sounds good . . . just like marriage.

My wife and I had just finished a course with our friends. This was our date night to celebrate with three other couples. I was thinking, *Bike riding, downtown, on the canal . . . this is gonna be a cool date!* Then we hopped on that tandem bike. All those nice feelings went away . . . quickly!

In tandem biking, much like marriage, fighting for control can end in disaster. What my wife found out pretty quickly was she had zero control while on the back of a tandem bike. What I quickly learned was I didn't have much control if I didn't help her feel comfortable while on the back of a tandem bike!

Tandem biking can be madness . . . just like marriage.

The biggest issue we had was in direct relation to our personalities. My goal was to make sure we got back safely. I wanted to see ahead, take my time, and enjoy the ride. My wife just wanted to ride out! To her this wasn't a joy ride but a thrill ride.

When I slowed to allow people to pass or move to the side, she felt I was breaking and resisted. I assumed she saw the people in front of us, but I learned after the ride she could see little. Many times she was unaware of what was happening in front. I'll be honest, at one point it got to be frustrating!

Tandem biking can be wonderful . . . just like marriage.

The frustration slowly began to go away after we reconnected with the other couples, and they shared their similar experiences.

The biggest lesson came when one couple shared their experience of trading places. When they began to see the ride from the other person's perspective, they began to understand what it was like to lead and what it was like to follow. Both were equally challenging.

In hindsight it was a test, but it was fun. I learned a few things about tandem bike riding and marriage.

1. *I learned you don't quit when it gets rough.* The first few minutes of our ride were tough. It was a challenge just getting on and getting started without hurting each other. But after we rode for a while, the ride became a little better. I'm sure the next time we ride we can enjoy it much more.
2. *I learned I needed to keep talking.* One of our biggest problems was a lack of communication. I assumed she knew when I was going to slow down and why. She had no idea and wondered (often loudly) why I was breaking. The couple that switched places shared how important it was to know what the other person was doing and why.
3. *I learned to stay in sync.* If she leaned left to look around me, the bike swayed. If she was pedaling when I was not, we

both began to lose control. But when we were both in sync and pedaling together, the ride was smooth.

4. *I learned to love the ride.* We can both say, in hindsight, the tandem bike ride was a great experience. We both wish we had taken the time to enjoy the ride a little more. The same goes with marriage. It may not be exactly as you expected, but the ride can be fun if you have the right perspective and work together. When you've weathered storms and persevered through hard times, you can enjoy a time to prosper.

(Note: If you haven't tried tandem biking, I suggest you do. Just make sure you have your counselor nearby or some good friends to help you through some of the issues that may come up as a result!)

Marriage Is the BOMB

Reminiscing about times like our unforgettable trip to Disney World and our crazy tandem bike-riding date makes me think about how thankful I am for my wife. When our marriage is Prospering, it's good (and easy) to look back and remember why we married each other in the first place. Sometimes I think, *I married her . . . I married Niecy Hogg (my wife's nickname plus maiden name).* I think, *WOW! I am a blessed man.* We've had our ups and downs, but I can say without a doubt, marriage is the bomb!

For those that know both my wife and me, and especially those who knew me back in the day, you can probably understand what I am about to say. I never thought I'd get married, and marriage never seriously crossed my mind. So for me to say, "I've been married fourteen years," is huge. And for me to be celebrating it with the person I am celebrating it with, is amazing!

The first and most obvious reason I married her is she is beautiful. Looking at her eyes and seeing her smile still does something to me to this day. She also is the most true, most caring, and most genuine-hearted person I have ever known.

I was a knucklehead before I met her and mostly "dated" the types of girls that date knuckleheads (so I dated some knucklehead-ettes?). However, she was different. Her spirit was gentle, yet strong. She was quiet, yet confident. She was graceful and bold at the same time. She was respectful but not to be messed with. She was a mix of many amazing qualities that together had me captivated. She still has me captivated today.

A few years ago we served in a ministry at our church called The B.O.M.B. Marriage Ministry. The acronym comes from Genesis 2:23:

> This one, at last, is *Bone Of My Bone* and flesh of my flesh; this one will be called "woman," for she was taken from man. (emphasis and capitals added)

That verse says so much. It represents a level of commitment that surpasses any relationship with any other person. And it is the reason our marriage is the bomb. Your marriage may be as well; if it is not, it can be. Here is my acronym of why our marriage is the BOMB and yours can be too.

- *Believers.* My wife and I are believers. First, we are believers in Jesus Christ and what He has done for us and in our lives. Second, we are believers in each other. My wife is not perfect, and I am so far away from perfect it is not funny. However, through our imperfections and mistakes we continue to believe in each other. And we feel secure in that.
- *One.* We are one. The verse talks about being flesh of my flesh, or *one flesh*. We take that seriously and live like it. If I do something to hurt my wife, I am actually hurting myself. If I do something to make my wife feel good, I am making myself feel good. We are one, and we do everything we can to preserve our oneness.
- *Make love.* I am going to be real. I have heard of married folks having sex once or twice per year. We make love regularly.

And staying 100 percent real, some of those times one of us does so even when not wanting to, just to please the other person. Remember, sex is the celebration of connecting spiritually, emotionally, and intellectually. You have to celebrate!

- *Best.* We truly want the best for each other. My wife is my number-one fan and supporter. Even though she knows everything about me. My faults, my fears, my weak areas. She still wants the best for me and does what she can to make it happen. And I am the same with her. And we prosper because of it. If you want a BOMB marriage, work for the best of everything in each other's lives.

Happy Husband

You and your spouse will wear all of the *7 Rings of Marriage* if you persevere. My wife and I have worn all seven rings. And all of them aren't pretty. Some are downright ugly, nasty, and just difficult. But this season, this ProspeRING of marriage is one of the best. Without a doubt, I can say (loudly) that I am a happy husband!

It is sad to me that so many couples don't make it to this point in their marriage. Many divorces happen in the first four years of marriage. Honestly, at four years you haven't even gotten started!

My marriage has shifted over the years from survival mode, to this marriage stuff is the BOMB, to I want all marriages to experience a great and happy marriage (more on that in the next chapter). But this ProspeRING season is all about wanting the best for your spouse and helping each other get there. So here are a few secrets I've learned along the way to being a happy husband.

1. *Know where your marriage is.* I have been pretty naive in our relationship at times. I wasn't always aware of what ring we were wearing. I always seemed to be caught up in the moment of trying to live, feed my family, and make things happen. But as we've grown and matured, I've been

more reflective. It has allowed me to see the big picture and understand the struggles we are facing at the time aren't our permanent situation. Sometimes my wife brings me to this realization. Knowing where we are in our marriage and that we are still growing has made me a happy husband.

2. *Be willing to be number two.* Without a doubt I do not come first in my wife's life. And neither do our kids or my mother-in-law. Her relationship with God comes before me, our kids, and everybody else. Because of this she can love and respect me through all my issues, which I have a lot. Having a wife who loves God above all else makes me a happy husband.

3. *Be a (prayer) warrior.* Sometimes we'll be sitting at the table, and all of a sudden I'll hear her over there mumbling something. I look up and she is praying. Praying because she received a request to pray for someone, or because something troubled her, or because the kids are acting crazy. I am not as big a prayer warrior as she is, but I love it, and I know the power in prayer. Having a praying wife makes me a happy husband.

4. *Never . . . ever, ever, ever . . . make it about you!* One of the biggest relationship killers is selfishness. I have an issue with it myself. Fortunately, I married one of the most selfless people you will ever come across. Honestly, sometimes her concern for others frustrates me because it puts her in bad positions. But I know without a doubt the genuine and selfless person that she is has made me a happy husband.

Loving Your Wife

Really, those secrets apply both to happy husbands and happy wives. But men, I want to take it a step further. Do you really want to love your wife and prosper in your marriage? The solution is simple. Do what Jesus did.

The "What Would Jesus Do?" bracelets were popular at one point. They raised a simple but thought-provoking question. A question that made you think deeper about the actions you were considering taking, or were in the midst of.

Our "endgame" in this life is to be more Christlike. In order to be more Christlike, we have to do our best to do what Jesus would do.

Jesus loved His bride. Husbands can do what Jesus did and love our brides; and when we do, our marriages will be lasting, powerful, and a great example for other marriages. Just like the relationship between Jesus and the church.

Guys, if your desire is to grow a better relationship with your wife, and to have a marriage that prospers, I encourage you to do what Jesus did in your marriage.

He gave up what was most important for Him when it conflicted with what was best for her, the church. Jesus made the ultimate sacrifice, His life. His life was important, probably more important than anything we are holding onto. The Bible shows us the conflicting emotions He had while praying in the garden of Gethsemane. *He didn't want to suffer, but He knew doing so would be the greatest blessing for His bride.*

He constantly built her up, and His relationship with her made her look even better. There was never a time when Jesus was not encouraging and building up the church. It was how He operated, and in doing so He made the church look better. Ephesians 5:27 says He makes the church look radiant (NIV). *Husbands, we should constantly encourage our wives, and the result will be beautiful.*

He took her with Him, and there was never a doubt she was His. When Jesus' ministry began, everything He did was for the church. He taught and preached constantly. If you saw Jesus in Jerusalem, He represented His bride. If you saw Him in the wilderness, with temptation, He represented His bride. *He left no doubt who His bride was.*

He left her in a great position when He died. I have heard count-less stories of a husband dying, and the family was completely unpre-pared, and it was traumatic on top of their grief. *When Jesus died, He left the church in a great position.* He prepared disciples for this time so they could continue sharing the message, and He left them with a resource that would meet their needs and comfort them. He left the Holy Spirit.

He covered His wife by praying for her. I am a firm believer that marriage is harder than it needs to be when we do not pray for and with our wives. Jesus constantly prayed. At the heart of His prayers was His bride. He prayed with the disciples, and He prayed alone. *Husbands, prayer with and for our wives should be nonnegotiable in our marriages.*

As husbands, when we constantly do what Jesus did in our mar-riages, we can make more of our days. I don't know about you, but when I think of what Jesus did on Good Friday, it touches me deeply. I know I am loved.

When your wife sees you loving her like Christ loved the church, she will be touched deeply. She will know she is loved.

Who Does the Housework?

Throughout my marriage I've done my best to study my wife and learn her likes, dislikes, turn-ons, and turnoffs. Sometimes (fre-quently) they change, and I have to unlearn or relearn her new likes, dislikes, turn-ons, and turnoffs!

Some of the fellas probably understand what I mean. But through all of that, one thing has consistently come back to me as an almost guaranteed way to energize our relationship. Being domestic sexy.

What in the world is "domestic sexy"? We all know what it means to be sexy. Attractive. Exciting. Appealing. Most of us relate the word *domestic* to work in and around the home or family. Household tasks such as cleaning, yard work, bathing the kids, or preparing meals. These tasks usually fall more on the side of the wife than the husband, although not always. When a husband is domestic sexy, he completes those tasks his wife normally does so she doesn't have to do them.

A domestic sexy husband handles the things his wife may be able to do. He also takes care of things that may be a little more challenging or undesirable to her such as household repairs, pumping gas, or cleaning the toilets. When you combine them, you get a husband who completes those tasks and is sexy to his wife. He is domestic sexy.

What happens when you are domestic sexy? First (and most obvious), things that need to be taken care of around your house are taken care of. But the impact it has is even greater.

It affects the *mental, emotional,* and *intimate* areas of your marriage. A domestic sexy action may be more appealing than flowers, more fulfilling than dinner out, and more relaxing than a back rub.

Mentally . . . your wife knows she is not in this alone. I have heard stories of wives who say they feel like they are single mothers, due to most of the burden of the domestic duties falling on them. When you are domestic sexy, your wife knows you are there for her and with her. She is secure in the fact that no matter what happens, you are going to do what is necessary to make sure she is comfortable.

Emotionally . . . your wife feels loved and feels you are truly concerned about her. This isn't a given in marriage. And even when it is present, we still must say and show it. As a husband, leave no doubt you love your wife! And remember, love is a verb; it is about action. Your actions as a domestic sexy husband will show you love your wife.

Intimately . . . your wife knows she has a strong chest to lay her head on. Although you may be grinding every day to provide for your family, you still have enough inside you to meet your wife's other needs. You want your wife to know when she is tired and falling, you are there to provide rest and to catch her. When she knows this, she will want to lay her head on you.

Many of us husbands are already doing the things mentioned above. For those who are, here is a fist bump and encouragement to keep it up. For the wives who have domestic sexy husbands, appreciate them and encourage them in word and action. I know I make all kinds of mistakes and mess things up, just like many other husbands, but when I am domestic sexy, it always invigorates our relationship.

More Than a Feeling

To close out this chapter, I want to share my one foolproof method I have found for Prospering in marriage. When you know and practice this in your marriage, it never fails. It is simple.

You must love your spouse.

Marriages that fail lack love. Yes, they lack love. You may be saying that is the reason couples get married. Love is what brought them together so, how can you say they lack love?

When I say *love*, I am not talking about the emotional, mushy, feeling of love. I am talking about real love. The love that never fails. The love God has for us. I emotionally love my wife. But sometimes that feeling can evaporate in a heartbeat!

I can come home after a hard day to find chaos and a mess. Feeling gone. I can be looking for my favorite shirt to wear only to find out of all the clothes washed, my shirt was somehow left at the bottom of the dirty hamper. Feeling gone.

The same goes for her. I can fall asleep before giving our boys a bath and leave it to her to finish after cooking and cleaning and homeschooling them all day. Feeling gone. I can drive her car and forget to put gas in it; then the next time she is rushing somewhere with the kids, she has to stop and pump gas. Feeling gone.

That feeling of love can come and go with your circumstances. However, the love that never fails isn't emotional and contingent on things or circumstances. It is a choice. It is doing. It is unconditional.

Even when you don't "feel it," you can choose to love your spouse to make your marriage prosper. The apostle Paul teaches us this principle in 1 Corinthians 13:4–8. He tells us what love is. Below I've listed ways to put this love into action.

- Be patient.
- Be kind.
- Do not envy.
- Do not boast.
- Do not be proud.
- Do not be rude.
- Do not be selfish.
- Don't keep a record of wrongs.

- Do not delight in evil.
- Rejoice with the truth.
- Always protect.
- Always trust.
- Always hope.
- Always persevere.
- Do not get easily angered.

When you and your spouse consistently do the actions of love, your marriage will never fail. Neglecting them can leave you subject to your emotions. When you are subject to your emotions, your marriage could become one of the negative statistics. That isn't what you planned. Are these actions present in your marriage? This is the kind of love that makes a marriage truly prosper.

Here are some questions to help you while wearing the ProspeRING:

1. When you were first married or as you are preparing for marriage, how did you envision this stage of marriage?
2. How can you begin to achieve it today?

Chapter Ten

Ring #7—MentoRING

"It's not the problem, but how you handle the problem."
–Author Unknown

I n marriage you go through good times, bad times, and ugly times. Sometimes it is hard to keep from generalizing your entire marriage based on a particular experience. We have to remember to keep those times in perspective.

When you have a bad or ugly marriage experience, you may find yourself using superlatives. "He *always*" . . . "She *never*" . . . "This is the *worst*." That is dangerous ground. Dangerous ground that leads to you not appreciating the good in your marriage and life.

As we learn about this last, and arguably most unique, ring of marriage, take a minute to give thanks for all those times—the good, the bad, and the ugly. Everything you've experienced so far in your marriage has prepared you to wear the MentoRING. Now that you've experienced hard times, good times, and everything in between, it's time to help other marriages that are walking down those same roads. It's time to give back.

Running on "Empty"

One morning, as we were preparing to leave home, my wife and I had a disagreement. Let me be real: it was a full-blown argument. Raising voices, laying blame, all of that. We were leaving in separate cars (not due to the argument) but going to the same place.

We left pretty angry at each other; well, I was really ticked off. To add to it, we were late, and we had to open the building so people were expecting us to be there.

Both vehicles needed gas, but the one I was driving was past "E." I left a minute or two before her to get gas. As I pulled up to the pump, I hear "Daddy." Apparently my wife had followed me.

She rolled down the window, had our daughter call my name, and my wife asked if she should get gas. I snapped back, "No!" and waved my hand for her to go ahead. You guys can beat me up later for not following my own advice here.

Immediately after that a guy came up to me. He had a mask on that covered everything but his eyes, and one of his eyes was covered with an eye patch. He was dressed pretty ratty. His clothes were dirty and torn in places. And he was driving a mo-ped in thirty-degree weather!

He introduced himself as Leon and told me he was driving to a job interview on the other side of town but had no gas. Remember, I am already ticked off and had just hollered at my wife. I was thinking, *Dude, I do not have time for this . . . and don't be rolling up on people like that!*

I had not checked our bank account and wasn't even sure if I had enough funds in our account to get gas for our cars. I told him that. I said if I have enough money after putting gas in my car, then I'll see if there is enough to put some in yours.

He began to share his story, and I began to ask him if he had a relationship with Jesus Christ. His story made my argument, anger, and issues pale in comparison to his.

He had a past drug problem, an illness which led to him losing his eye. He of course was broke but had this opportunity to get a job to help. His mother had recently passed, but he shared that she accepted Jesus Christ before she died.

After pumping my gas, I filled his tank, not even sure if it would clear my account. I prayed with him, and we went our separate ways.

I may never see him again, and I cannot verify his story. But I think our encounter was just as much about me as it was about his getting gas money and prayer. When I left, my attitude took a complete 180-degree turn.

Before, I was angry with my wife, using superlatives, and just making more out of the situation than was necessary. As I reflected on it all, a few things came to my mind about perspective in our marriage. These three things can be helpful for all our marriages but especially if you are wearing the MentoRING.

1. *Our marriage is on display.* Marriage is the most private public thing there is. Meaning, many of the things we do in marriage are done behind closed doors and personal to our own marriage. Yet, the fruit, the results, are shown in full view to those we cross paths with. Leon probably wasn't the only person who saw my interaction with my wife. Fortunately, he didn't let it stop him from approaching me.

2. *Our marriage should be viewed through a wider lens.* At the time I crossed paths with Leon, I was viewing my marriage in a narrow lens. The lens of the argument we had just had. All my actions were following suit. Had Leon not been looking so rough, I might have snapped at him. His appearance had me being a little cautious initially. But after our conversation I began to look at the big picture. Our marriage and our situation didn't look so bad.

3. *There is purpose to everything in our marriages.* I am not sure the argument we had was purposeful in the encounter with Leon. However, I know each experience gives us an opportunity to grow. Each experience provides us a chance to display something good with our marriage. We don't always know what that is, but keeping

this perspective will help us handle good, bad, and ugly experiences better.

Example for Your Kids

The first place this Mentoring happens has to be in the home. Once you have children, your life changes. You begin to do things differently in an effort to care for, provide, and guide your children. Of all those things, a father can do one thing that will provide the greatest impact on his children's lives.

The single greatest thing a dad can do for his children is to love their mother. Plain and simple!

When the kids see dad loving mom, then they see what love looks like. Your sons will know how to relate to women as they grow older. Your daughters will know how a man should talk to her and how a man should treat her. Nothing less will be acceptable.

Loving your children's mother frees her to love and nurture them. Your love encourages and inspires her to do so in the best way she can. Nothing should be allowed to get in the way of this love being expressed to them. *Now the love of your children is exponential,* and you are having an impact well beyond your marriage.

Peace comes in the household when dad loves mom. When you love someone, you care that their needs are met as much as you care that your needs are met. You make a constant effort to meet the other person's needs. Anytime mom's and dad's needs are met, the children's needs usually are too.

We can do much more when we work with others striving for the same thing. Our children feel the bond of a team and know if they falter there is not just one person to pick them up but two people working together to get them back on track. That team is a wonderful foundation that much can be built from.

I encourage all my fellow fathers not just to love your children but to *love your wives, love the mothers of your children.* You will create a solid foundation for your children that will provide lifelong benefits, greater than anything else!

Role Models

Marriage role models. That's what we are. To our kids. To singles. To other married couples. Whether you like it or not, when you are married, you are a *role model.* The question is: Are you a good role model or a bad role model?

As a kid I always had an athlete I wanted to be like. Somebody I looked up to. When I became an adult, I began looking up to successful entrepreneurs. Sports were my biggest interest as a kid and entrepreneurship one of my biggest as an adult. So naturally I looked to those who did it best, who were successful, and who really loved what they did.

But what about marriage? Vastly more people get married than go pro in a sport. The same can be said for entrepreneurs. Yet, have you seen or heard a child say, "When I grow up, I want to be a husband just like that!" You may argue that many young girls have a desire to get married, but do they have a "wife role model"?

Take Responsibility

Some debate whether athletes or entertainers should be considered role models. I'm not sure, but they are thrust in the spotlight and into the *role model* position so with that does come a level of responsibility. The same goes for marriage.

Whether married couples like it or not, other people are watching your marriage. Your coworkers, your friends, other married couples, singles, and most important, your kids. When you commit to marriage, you have a responsibility. First to God, your wife, and the children you bring into that marriage. Then you have responsibility to everyone else looking at your marriage.

Model Marriage

If your kids are to play and be passionate about sports, you have to expose them to it. Take them to games, practice with them, sign them up for a league, talk to them about the sport. If your kids are to have someone to look up to in marriage, you have to expose them to a marriage worth looking up to. That should be *your* marriage.

Model dating after marriage. Model communication when you agree and disagree. Model joy and happiness. Model problem-solving. Model money management. Model learning. Model trust and respect.

"Nobody Told Me"

More than likely your kids are going to get married some day. When they do, you want them to be as prepared as possible for what marriage brings. The good and the bad. If you are married, at some point you've probably said, *"Nobody told me it would be like this!"* We prepare our kids for almost everything else. Marriage should be included in that.

I don't want our kids ever to be able to say, "Nobody told me." Just like everything else in life, I want them to be as prepared as possible for marriage. I may not be able to prepare them for everything, but I will do my best to equip them to handle everything as best they can. And if they have a marriage like ours, then they can feel comfortable they can live with that.

What Are Your Qualifications?

If you think all the way back to chapter 2, I asked you to commit to saying no and yes to your marriage. No to divorce and yes to your marriage being a ministry. Your marriage is an opportunity to minister to others. You have the opportunity to share your marriage with others, and you could be the couple that says or does something to help restore hope in a couple or to encourage them as they are working to grow together in their marriage.

What opportunities do you have to share your marriage? Couples date nights? Counseling others? Have you been invited to speak at your church or in a marriage class? Can you write your story and share it with others online?

Do you feel qualified to use your marriage as a ministry? Before you get ahead of yourself and think, *No*, let me tell you, I've felt the same way. Sometimes I think back and wonder, *How did I ever get here? How did I get to the point of writing not only blog posts, and doing interviews, but writing a book and a marriage curriculum in partnership with one of the largest and most influential publishing companies there is?* It doesn't make sense to me sometimes, and honestly throughout me writing this book, I had constant doubts I was the right person. I kept thinking, *They chose the wrong person.* I can't help anybody when it comes to their marriage. The fact that you are reading this book and have made it this far in the book says something different. It's humbling and an honor to hopefully put the words on paper that have the power to transform someone else's marriage and life.

I'm only qualified because I've been humbled before. I've been humbled by years of marriage challenges and relationship mistakes. I remember the time when we were in our church's new member class with our three-month-old daughter in the "bucket carrier," and the minister teaching the class called to us in the back of the room and asked how many years we were married. I answered, "We aren't married." Although I knew we should be based on how we were functioning. Ironically that same minister asked us a few years later to play a prominent role in our church's brand-new marriage ministry, and he is now someone we consider family. My wife and I, as well as our kids, call him, "Uncle." Being humbled like that has enabled us to relate to the couple that is experiencing what we experienced years ago.

I alluded to our unforgettable honeymoon at the beginning of the book. We could only afford to go to a state park a few hours south of Indianapolis, and it ended up being a total disaster. We were late, as typical for us, so we arrived at dark. Our "honeymoon suite" was a small log cabin in the middle of this park filled with all kinds of creatures. Neither Stephana nor I are big outdoors people, so it wasn't pretty. We actually almost turned back because when we pulled up to our cabin, we heard this screeching or squealing that sounded like it was straight out of a horror flick. No cars, no lights, no people, and we pull up to our little ole cabin to hear some crazy sounds like that. It was my first test of "being a man" for my family, as my dad told me on my wedding day. We finally found out, thankfully before I had to get out of the car to check, that it was a cat in heat. It didn't get better as our bed was not clean enough for Stephana to sleep on so she slept on the couch. The best part was riding bikes up and down the large hills (Stephana loves to ride bikes), but fighting the bugs when we got done was not good. Just like eating the fried chicken we bought from some fast-food restaurant was not. Having a start to our marriage that wasn't fairy-tale has enabled us to speak on the same level as a couple who may wish things had started differently in their relationship.

I remember the guilt and stupidity I felt when I saw our cordless phone in pieces on the floor after a "disagreement" that turned into a shouting, screaming, slamming doors, and throwing stuff showdown. I never knew how much anger I had pent up inside of me until we experienced disagreements, problems, or "spilled milk" in the first few years of our marriage. I was so frustrated and so unable to voice my concerns and frustrations in words that I literally got violent against that poor phone and threw it against the wall. And I used to be a pretty good baseball player so I didn't just toss it; I threw that phone like I was trying to throw the game-winning runner out at home plate. I couldn't believe I was capable of that, and even more, I couldn't believe how dumb that was. Up to that point, I'd never really had conflict like that in a relationship that I couldn't just walk away. Back in the day, if a girlfriend made me so mad, or I allowed myself to get so mad, that I resorted to yelling, screaming, and throwing stuff, then I would be done with the relationship. I never got beyond that point because I never cared enough about another person to commit. But I committed to my wife and our marriage. And I got angry when things weren't going my way, after all she committed to me too! Because I've done things I couldn't believe I'd ever do, things that actually scared me, it enables me and my wife to relate to couples who are there now.

I remember the bad news from the doctor about the likelihood of one of our kids being born with a birth defect based on some findings during the ultrasound. I remember waking up to my wife's crying, holding our lifeless son (toddler at the time) in her arms after he had a seizure, and a repeat of that a few months later, and all the ER trips and exams, and scans and the concern for him and his health. I remember our daughter's dealing with transient tics and her doctor saying if it keeps up for twelve months she'd be diagnosed with Tourette's syndrome if she didn't grow out of it. Having a sick child, receiving a bad doctor report, or dealing with anything seemingly out of your control can rock your marriage. We've experienced it. We've had the concerns. We've spent late nights crying and praying. Because God allowed us to go through these things, we can encourage those who are going through them now.

I remember quickly placing our furniture, clothing, and belongings into the U-Haul, and while doing so, quickly having to decide whether it was (1) keeper, (2) storage, or (3) trash. Then after multiple trips to drop off items to our storage unit and take trash to the dumpster, returning to depressingly discover still more work than we could handle. In addition there was what seemed like a mountain of garbage outside getting rained on, that we'd have to put in the back of our car and take to the dumpster because the U-Haul was full. Then for the next few months living between basement floors, spare bedrooms, hotels, corporate housing apartments, and the storage unit where 90 percent of our stuff was. A few times per week, while I worked, my wife would have to take a trip with the kids to the storage unit to dig through boxes, bags, and stacks of items to find clothes, shoes, and other items we needed. She'd have to go through boxes of school supplies that were needed for our homeschooling groups' science and art projects. I'd be hustling to create the income needed to pay our storage fees each month. Yet I also remember our kids playing games, finding "new" toys, and having a ball during those storage trips. All of it was humbling, but it also stripped us of our ideas of what was truly valuable. It, too, enabled us to help other couples that have experienced times like these.

All of my memories and things that have prepared us to mentor other couples aren't bad. I remember being in the delivery room for each of our three kids and the joy and excitement we both shared when our kids were born. I remember watching our daughter perform in a play when she was four years old that had people gasping because of the length and depth of all she memorized for that part. Her memorization skills developed in part from one or both of us reading her the same children's Bible almost every night before bed for the first two to three years of her life. I remember our son being born, 100 percent healthy, after all the negative doctor reports were saying it was highly possible he'd have a birth defect.

I remember going to concerts with Stephana and feeling like we were falling in love all over again. I remember hanging out with the couples in our small group enjoying various couples' exercises and activities that were geared to build our relationship but were so much fun to do. I remember the trip to the mountains in Tennessee with this same group of couples from our small group and "skiing," or skiing for twenty feet before baseball sliding to stop myself, and enjoying each other alone in the cabin, as well as the company of other couples. I remember our first marriage retreat where we took a bus trip to Chicago, and all the other couples were teasing us because they thought we both looked fourteen years old, and we weren't supposed to be on the trip.

Through our marriage we've experienced a lot, including all *7 Rings of Marriage*, and I'm willing to bet you have too. Don't let your problems or challenges deter you from helping that couple, or from joining that ministry, or from accepting that opportunity to speak to a group about marriage. Every single thing we've gone through in our relationship to this point in some way has equipped us to help someone else. We finally recognized this, and we finally chose to move forward with it. Now it's your turn.

Here are some questions to help you while wearing the MentoRING:

1. What experience of yours can you share to encourage another marriage?
2. Whom can you begin to pour into and encourage in their marriage today?

Chapter Eleven

What Ring Are You Wearing?

"There is joy in the journey."
−Author Unkown

T he State of the Union is an annual address by the president of the United States to a joint session of Congress. The purpose of the address is to provide a report on the condition of our nation while allowing presidents to outline their plans and priorities.

No matter who is in office, there is always a wide range of opinions on how well our country is doing. I've yet to see one president deliver this address without an opposing opinion. It comes with the territory. But what happens when you believe your marriage is in great condition, but your wife doesn't? Or vice versa?

I've been there and know of many other couples that have as well. No matter how hard it may be to come to the realization that our marriages are not as great as we thought, it needs to be addressed.

As couples, just like our government, we need to address where our marriage is and where it's going. And we need to do it together. Here are some ways you can assess the state of your union and make sure it's heading in a direction that pleases you and your spouse.

1. *Ask questions.* One of the best ways to learn the state of your union is to ask your spouse.
2. *Get counseling.* Counseling isn't only for marriages on the brink of divorce. Bringing in an experienced person or couple can help you determine the state of your marriage.
3. *Get away.* My wife and I attend a marriage retreat every single year. We learn something about each other and/or our marriage each time.
4. *Ask someone close to you.* Sometimes we don't see what is really happening because we are in the middle of it. Asking a close friend or family member you trust can help you see things you don't.
5. *Start journaling.* Every couple should journal their marriage experiences. When you regularly journal and reflect, you will see themes, reoccurring challenges, and even solutions to problems that can help you today.
6. *Date regularly.* Spending time together, especially date nights, will provide a regular outlet to communicate without kids, work, and household duties. Focused time can bring clarity.
7. *Pray daily.* Prayer time is intimate. When my wife and I pray together, we intimately see each other in ways we've never seen. Praying together exposes what's really going on inside.

Marriages that end in divorce don't do so in an instant. It's a gradual process that eventually leads to the point of no return in a couple's mind. Regularly assessing the state of your union can bring awareness to challenges or potential problems that can be addressed and fixed, if needed. It can also reveal some great things in your marriage as well.

Below are forty-nine statements. Seven statements for each of the *7 Rings of Marriage*. Please circle the number you agree best describes your feelings and experiences in relation to your marriage today. For the statements that you feel the strongest about, circle the number 5. Those you feel least likely relate to your marriage today, circle the number 1.

Engagement RING

1. We have no boundaries or basis for making decisions in our marriage.
   Disagree   1   2   3   4   5   Agree

2. Maybe now is the time to bring God into our relationship.
   Disagree   1   2   3   4   5   Agree

3. We aren't on the same page spiritually when it comes to our relationship.
   Disagree   1   2   3   4   5   Agree

4. I'm not sure we know what marriage is really about.
   Disagree   1   2   3   4   5   Agree

5. I feel like we were lovers before becoming friends.
   Disagree   1   2   3   4   5   Agree

6. Our marriage could be much better had we done some things different early in our relationship.
   Disagree   1   2   3   4   5   Agree

7. I thought his/her personality indicated some relational challenges that I should have addressed before now.
   Disagree   1   2   3   4   5   Agree

Wedding RING

1. Every time I see him/her my heart races.
    Disagree   1   2   3   4   5   Agree

2. Now I think I know what head over heels in love feels like.
    Disagree   1   2   3   4   5   Agree

3. I don't know what our future together holds, but it's really exciting.
    Disagree   1   2   3   4   5   Agree

4. I understand we need to plan for our future, but we are having the time of our lives right now.
    Disagree   1   2   3   4   5   Agree

5. I'm not 100 percent comfortable with sharing everything.
    Disagree   1   2   3   4   5   Agree

6. He/she shouldn't have issues with doing things the way my parents did in their marriage.
    Disagree   1   2   3   4   5   Agree

7. My before-marriage friends are cool, and I don't see any issues with hanging out with them as I've always done.
    Disagree   1   2   3   4   5   Agree

DiscoverRING

1. It's exciting peeling back the layers of my spouse and learning more about him/her.
    Disagree   1   2   3   4   5   Agree

2. We are experiencing things I could not have predicted in our marriage.
    Disagree   1   2   3   4   5   Agree

3. This is not what I thought being married to him/her would be like.
    Disagree   1   2   3   4   5   Agree

4. I'm really enjoying doing new things with him/her.
Disagree   1   2   3   4   5   Agree

5. There's something about him/her that I just can't put my finger on.
Disagree   1   2   3   4   5   Agree

6. I can't believe he/she never told me that.
Disagree   1   2   3   4   5   Agree

7. Wow, I never knew how many issues I had or how selfish I could be.
Disagree   1   2   3   4   5   Agree

PerseveRING

1. I am hurt, deeply hurt, and I have no idea what to do.
Disagree   1   2   3   4   5   Agree

2. We are constantly having problems and are at odds with each other.
Disagree   1   2   3   4   5   Agree

3. I feel so alone in our marriage, even when we are together.
Disagree   1   2   3   4   5   Agree

4. I want out of this marriage.
Disagree   1   2   3   4   5   Agree

5. My physical, emotional, or intellectual needs are not being met.
Disagree   1   2   3   4   5   Agree

6. Something that one of us has recently done, or said, has changed our marriage forever.
Disagree   1   2   3   4   5   Agree

7. We are facing one of the biggest challenges we've ever faced in our lives right now.
Disagree   1   2   3   4   5   Agree

RestoRING

1. I'm not sure if I'll ever be able to get past what has happened.
   Disagree   1   2   3   4   5   Agree

2. We have unforgiveness and bitterness between us.
   Disagree   1   2   3   4   5   Agree

3. We made it through a rough patch, and now I'm excited to see how it grows our relationship.
   Disagree   1   2   3   4   5   Agree

4. I often think about what we can do to bring back the love, excitement, and fun we had before.
   Disagree   1   2   3   4   5   Agree

5. I often find myself confused as to why something (bad) happened, but I'm determined to find purpose in it.
   Disagree   1   2   3   4   5   Agree

6. This problem is bigger than us. We need help in a major way.
   Disagree   1   2   3   4   5   Agree

7. I have no idea how we allowed ourselves to get here, but we have to fix it.
   Disagree   1   2   3   4   5   Agree

ProspeRING

1. We rarely have challenges or disagreements that linger for days.
   Disagree   1   2   3   4   5   Agree

2. He/she pushes my buttons, but I understand he/she loves me and is doing his/her best.
   Disagree   1   2   3   4   5   Agree

3. I can't think of anything greater than what we're experiencing in our relationship right now.
   Disagree   1   2   3   4   5   Agree

4. What used to really irk me about him/her doesn't seem to have the same impact anymore.
Disagree   1   2   3   4   5   Agree

5. If I could do it (our marriage) over again, I wouldn't change a thing.
Disagree   1   2   3   4   5   Agree

6. We are facing a huge problem, but I know we'll make it through together without a doubt.
Disagree   1   2   3   4   5   Agree

7. I can now say I've experienced true unconditional love.
Disagree   1   2   3   4   5   Agree

MentoRING

1. I wonder how our marriage impacts others.
Disagree   1   2   3   4   5   Agree

2. Modeling a great marriage to our kids seems important right now.
Disagree   1   2   3   4   5   Agree

3. Other couples seek our advice and help for their marriage.
Disagree   1   2   3   4   5   Agree

4. We are chosen to speak or serve in marriage ministries and enrichment activities.
Disagree   1   2   3   4   5   Agree

5. I often think of what great purpose God has for all we've experienced in our marriage.
Disagree   1   2   3   4   5   Agree

6. We clearly see what a great platform and opportunity to minister to others we have in our marriage.
Disagree   1   2   3   4   5   Agree

7. It hurts me deeply when I see other couples struggling in their
    marriage or hear about the couples who get divorced.
    Disagree   1   2   3   4   5   Agree

Add up your numbers and write the totals in their respective
spaces below. The highest score you can receive for any one ring is
thirty-five. The lowest is seven.

Engagement RING: _____
Wedding RING: _____
DiscoveRING: _____
PersveRING: _____
RestoRING: _____
ProspeRING: _____
MentoRING: _____

Determining What Ring You Are Wearing Today

The ring you are currently wearing is the one that received the
highest score. It is possible to be wearing more than one ring if you
have more than one ring with the same high score. If your second
highest score is very close to your highest, don't neglect it because it
didn't finish at the top. There is no wrong score, or bad score. It is
just an indicator of what ring you are wearing and what you can
focus on during this season of your marriage.

The benefit is now you know what might be potential problems,
what you can do to best strengthen your marriage, and what you
can do to continue growing and moving to your lasting and more
fulfilling marriage. If you happen to score the same amount for each
ring, then I suggest you start working on your foundation, which
the Engagement RING focuses on. You may have yourself wearing
particular rings more than once over the course of your marriage.
When this happens you are more equipped to make the most of it

the subsequent time(s), and reach even more fulfillment as you have been there and done that.

If you took this assessment alone, encourage your spouse to take it as well. Knowing where you both stand and what both of your perceptions are of the state of your union will help you better relate, and better understand one another. With the ultimate goal of having a lasting and a truly fulfilling marriage.

One more thing: make sure you go to jackiebledsoe.com/ 7ringsbonuses to get all the extra free marriage resources to keep you moving toward your lasting and fulfilling marriage.

Chapter Twelve

End with the Beginning

*"Put and keep your marriage in the forefront
of your mind to keep it moving forward"*
–Author Unkown

O n our web show we always ask couples if they have ever faced a time in their marriage when they felt stuck. Meaning have they ever felt like they were stuck with their spouse in a negative sense, or just stuck in a particular season of their marriage.

Most couples say they have never felt stuck in a negative sense with their spouse, but just about all of them say they've been stuck in a particular season. We've been there plenty of times, and sometimes we've felt like after getting unstuck we've gone right back to being stuck.

Now that you know which ring you are wearing, you may be elated about the season of marriage you're in, or you may feel stuck, wishing you could hurry up and move on to the next ring. No matter where or how you're stuck, it is frustrating and can lead you to a point where you lose hope in your marriage, in your spouse, or even in yourself. Once hope is lost, you are in a scary place.

When you get stuck and a loss of hope results, you may self-sabotage your marriage in many ways. When I first shared the *7 Rings,* that was one of the things I picked up from all the positive feedback the original blog post received. It gave couples hope. Couples could relate because they could determine where they were in their marriage, and they could see that they were not alone. Other couples had been there, will be there, or are currently there. I want you to have hope that your marriage can last and it can be fulfilling. Then you can take intentional actions that help you versus self-sabotaging actions that hurt you.

One of the biggest things to remember when it comes to your hope is who your hope is in. If your hope is in your husband or your wife, then your hope will fail. You and your spouse are flawed and imperfect. We let ourselves down so we will definitely let our spouses down. Our hope has to be firmly planted in Jesus Christ.

"'For I know the plans I have for you'—this is the LORD's declaration—'plans for your welfare, not for disaster, to give you a future and a hope'" (Jer. 29:11).

Our hope is with Christ, and this hope is where we'll find the strength to push through seasons where we find our marriages stuck. Even when you're facing seemingly insurmountable challenges, your hope can be restored.

"Return to a stronghold, you prisoners who have hope; today I declare that I will restore double to you" (Zech. 9:12).

That is your first step to getting unstuck. It is placing your hope in something, or Someone, who is incapable of failing you. Something you can stand on or cling to when you have nothing else or nobody else to depend on. Marriage gets that way, especially when you are stuck and losing hope. I'm ensuring that when you place your hope in Jesus Christ your marriage is setting course to experience everything you dreamed of and that will ultimately last and fulfill both you and your spouse.

Choose How Your Marriage Will End

One of the biggest lessons I've learned in my life is also applicable in my marriage. It is the lesson of being intentional. Things just don't happen by accident. Not the forming of the earth, not the success of an organization, not the creation of a product or service, and definitely not the success of a marriage.

The couples that have lasting and fulfilling marriages did some things on purpose to get where they are. First they made a decision. A decision to stay in their marriage and a decision to make their marriage the best it can be.

Then they became intentional about making their marriage amazing. That's what Stephana and I have done over the years. We've been intentional about working toward a better marriage. We have never been perfect, but we have been intentional in moving in the direction we want to go. You won't always necessarily move through *7 Rings of Marriage* in order, and sometimes you will go back to an earlier ring. That's okay as long as you are always moving toward your marriage goals.

There is no lukewarm to your marriage. It's either hot like fire or cold like ice. Whether you are intentional or not will tell you how you've chosen your marriage will end. As I mentioned earlier in the book, you have two primary ways your marriage will end. In death (until death do us part) or in divorce. You have to decide today—no, right now. How will my marriage end? Once your mind wraps around that, you'll find yourself taking steps toward it. Sometimes it will be harder than others, but you have the capacity to endure if you choose, if you wrap your mind around it.

Before we close out our journey together, I want to leave you with ideas on how you can put all this into action. Because the end of this book means the beginning of the marriage you've always dreamed was possible. At the start of this book, we talked about what marriage is really for and the purpose. Now you know, you've assessed your marriage, you've identified which ring you are currently wearing. Now what? How can you take real, intentional steps toward putting your marriage success plan into action and having the most amazing marriage possible? What can you do right now, today, to get you one step closer to your goal? That's what I want to share in this chapter. Pick just one of these, any one, put it into action today, and you will start to see results.

Do Something Different

Sometimes you get so busy and so focused on accomplishing things (even good things) that you forget to focus on the relationships in your life. One particular season I was guilty as charged. A lot was going on in our household, and I had some goals and deadlines to meet over the next several weeks. My focus and much of my time had been there, and I hadn't spent as much quality time as I would have liked with my wife. When this happens, it is tough to function. I'm sure she would say I am tough to deal with!

So this led me to think about what I could do to get back in the right direction and get the most out of what God has for us in our marriage. If you want different results, you usually have to do something different! There is purpose in our marriage, and I want to make it count. Below are some things I committed to do for a period of seven days to get us back on track. These were seven ways I identified that I could bless my spouse and move us closer to our marriage goals. The list is geared toward husbands, but it applies to the wife's perspective as well. Also, notice that all can be done without spending a dime!

1. *Apologize to her (or him).* Husbands, just like me, you have done something wrong in the past seven days. Find out what it is and apologize. Even if you don't know what it is, apologize.

2. *Focus on her (or him).* Spend thirty minutes communicating without any distractions. Nothing but you and your spouse. No phones, no computers, no TV, no kids, no music, nothing but the two of you. (Note: Do more listening than talking.)

3. *Feed her (or him).* Plan, prepare, serve, and clean up a meal specifically for your spouse. Make something your spouse likes a lot. Husbands, if you don't have the skills to prepare her "favorite dish," then try for "her favorite dish that you can pull off."

4. *Leave her (or him).* Set up a time where your spouse can spend a few hours of time to herself. If you have kids, then take the kids somewhere and stay gone for a preset period of time. If she prefers to be out of the house, then help her plan or make arrangements.

5. *Join her (or him).* Find out one thing your spouse really likes to do and do it with her. If she has a favorite TV show, watch it with her. Favorite hobby or activity, do it with her. Just make sure you do it on her terms. (If she likes silence during the show, then no talking!)

6. *Relieve her (or him).* Your spouse has a thousand things to do this week, and a million things on her mind. Provide a break for your spouse by taking on at least one thing she normally does.

7. *Compliment her (or him).* Every day, every week, every month your spouse does things you appreciate but say nothing. Look for opportunities to compliment your wife (or husband) on these everyday things, not just the "big" things.

GET What You Want out of Marriage

I'll be honest, sometimes I want to get what I want in marriage. It sounds selfish, but I'm keeping it real. In spite of my "realness," I know, and you do too, that marriage isn't about me (or you).

Your happiness in marriage will depend on how well you meet the needs of your spouse.

If you don't understand the point above, then you are in for a bumpy ride. When you do understand it, you can fully embrace getting what you want in marriage, and you can do it without being completely selfish!

So, how is it done? How can you get what you want in marriage? It is actually pretty simple.

Give

The first "trick" to getting what you want is giving. It is plain and simple: when you give, you will receive. It's proven and it's biblical. Luke 6:38 reads, "Give, and it will be given to you." Proverbs 11:24 reads, "One person gives freely, yet gains more; another withholds what is right, only to become poor." So not only will you benefit by giving; if you do not give, you will suffer.

If you want respect, then give respect to your spouse. If you want quality time, then pay attention when they are talking. Intimacy? A back or foot massage every now and again won't hurt.

However, do not give with the sole purpose of getting something in return. Give because you want your spouse to know you love them, respect them, and they are important to you. Give and you shall receive.

Encourage

Encouraging words can do wonders for a person. They are refreshing, and I would say the phrase "too much of a good thing" does not apply here. The Bible says, "Kind words are like honey. They are sweet to the spirit and bring healing to the body" (Prov. 16:24 NIRV). They bring healing to the body. Wow!

If you want to get what you want in marriage, bring some healing to your spouse's aching body in the form of encouraging words.

I relate this to someone smiling at you. It is hard not to return the smile. That smile does something to you: it makes you feel good; it makes you want someone else to feel just as good.

Encouraging words will bring a sweetness and healing to your relationship.

Teach

I have coached youth sports for the past eight years and taught middle school kids for the past two years. One thing that has stood out to me is this: the more I teach, the more I learn. When you study something for yourself, you get some understanding. However, when you study something to help someone else, you gain *a lot* of understanding.

That has been my experience with coaching, teaching, and now writing. I write for myself and my readers. Through my efforts to teach what I've learned from my experiences, my marriage is benefiting, my parenting skills are improving, and my family is being blessed.

Maybe you don't coach, teach, or write, but there is some family, some married couple, with less experience than you that you can come alongside to help. Teaching has helped me get more of what I want, and it can do the same for you.

If you are intentional in your giving, encouraging, and teaching, I'm certain you can get what you want in your marriage. You will benefit, and so will those you come in contact with.

Planting Seeds

After looking at my marriage and all we'd gone through—good and bad—I can clearly see how each of the *7 Rings of Marriage* is common in every marriage relationship.

I think one reason the *7 Rings* have been so impactful is because people could find their relationship within at least one of the rings, and most had gone through a few rings already. There is comfort in knowing what we go through is normal and others go through this. There's also an added comfort seeing what is to come when you stay the course.

It's similar to seed planting. Indiana weather is notoriously unpredictable, so it could be sunny now and start snowing by the time you finish this chapter. The weather has an impact, but primarily there are specific seasons when seeds need to be planted. You have to get seeds in the ground when it's ready for them.

Although during certain times of the year the ground is ready for the seeds, the ground will not immediately produce what it's supposed to produce from that seed. That will come later, maybe. It will only produce what is hoped for if we do something daily to help it grow.

If we don't water it regularly, let it get light, protect it from predators, or prune the things around it which can impact its growth, then it won't happen. Does that sound like a marriage? It is just like a marriage. There is a season of planting and a season of harvesting.

When your expectations are a harvest during the season of planting or nurturing, frustration will come. The thing about a marriage is it is always in a season of planting and nurturing. Some seasons, or some "rings," you'll do more seed planting than others, but you should never stop. Here are three seeds you can begin planting today to lead you to a season of harvest:

1. *Kind words.* Your words are seeds no matter if they are kind or not. But remember, you can't get a pear from an apple seed.
2. *Acts of service.* Don't limit your seed planting to words. Show your love in action.
3. *Acts of grace.* Your spouse is not perfect. Don't treat them like they are. When they mess up, show some grace.

Protect and Nurture

It's easy to get stuck and lose hope of your dreams of happily ever after. You expected to date, fall in love, get married, buy a house, have kids, and happily ever after would soon follow. Now you know that isn't always the way it happens. Sometimes it seems you spend more time fighting off the 50 percent divorce rate hanging over our heads than being happy. At least we felt that way at times. We spent a lot of years fighting to stay together before we changed our fight to fulfillment and now helping other couples. It's a better fight.

Things, people, and circumstances can bring even the most prospering marriage down if you are not careful. For me as a husband, God has called me to be the head, the priest, the first line of defense, the sacrificial lamb, the "whatever" is needed to cover and protect Stephana and the kids. Anything that goes down, good or bad, in our marriage begins with me. I accept this. But it doesn't mean I am fighting alone.

Men naturally look for a fight or something to compete for or something to protect. Women naturally look to find something or some way to nurture. That comes naturally to most. To keep your marriage from remaining stuck, you need both. You need to fight off challenges and protect your union. But you also need to nurture it so it can grow. Pick your battles. There are certain areas you should focus on to give you the most results when it comes to protecting and nurturing your marriage. Here are the areas that require our utmost attention and focus.

Spiritual

Spiritual warfare is real and is the first place of protection. You will be amazed at how things change when you are in a right relationship with Christ. The reason they change is because you change first. If this area is not protected and nurtured, it becomes more challenging to do so in the other areas. If this area is protected and nurtured, it becomes easier to do so in the other areas.

Time

Technology advancements are supposed to make us more productive. Sometimes I think they just make us busier. With so many time sucks, the time with our spouses needs to be protected and nurtured . . . and that includes from our own kids. Mommy/Daddy time or husband/wife time must be nonnegotiable, and everyone else must know and respect it!

Physical

Of course if somebody approaches our wives in a threatening way, we are going to step up to them. But what about the health of our wives or the health of your husbands, ladies? I personally want a long and high-quality life with my wife. I know we have to take care of our health in terms of what we eat, getting active, and resting our bodies properly for that to happen. Encourage your spouse; take a leading role in living a healthy life together.

Relationships

We all come into marriage with different ideas and expectations. Many are learned from our parents or the other marriages we've witnessed. Some of those expectations need to be unlearned. And unfortunately, some relationships need to be let go. If a relationship comes between you and your spouse, then guess what? That relationship needs to go! I am not saying cut off your family and friends, but you don't have to live your marriage like theirs. Leave and cleave to your spouse.

Finances

This is one of the main reasons many marriages end in divorce. One of you may be the analytical person, numbers person, and enjoy it all. While the other may be able to see the big picture and some potential areas that may trip you up and keep you from reaching your goals. Both spouses should be informed and involved in your finances. For us I am the visionary, I look out and see what threats are out on the horizon. But sometimes I'm so busy looking out and looking ahead that I may miss things right in front of me. That's where Stephana comes in to nurture the execution of our plan. We manage our finances best when both of us play an active part.

These are some areas that take practical action to keep your marriage growing and moving forward.

Healthy Marriages

Some rings or seasons of your marriage will be smooth sailing. Others will be trying and challenging. But no matter what ring you are currently wearing, you can have a healthy marriage. You can be DiscoveRING and have a healthy marriage. You can be PerseveRING the toughest storms of your life and still have a healthy marriage.

Do you have a healthy marriage now? If you were to have a marriage checkup, what would the physician prescribe? Just as our bodies can be in good or bad health, our marriages can be as well. Having a healthy marriage isn't much different from having a healthy body.

When we address our physical health, we typically focus on three areas: *nutrition, cardio,* and *strength training.* When these areas are addressed, the result is a healthy body. *So how does that relate to a healthy marriage?*

Boundaries (Nutrition)

When it comes to nutrition, some foods are good for our body and some aren't, and the same applies to our marriage. There are just some things we cannot allow in. In our marriage we need to set up three main boundaries: (1) never use the "D" word (divorce) or the threat of leaving the relationship; (2) never let an outside influence cause an internal problem; and (3) never walk out in the middle of an argument. Just as sugar, refined foods, and caffeine can be toxic to our bodies, certain things can be toxic to our marriage. Don't allow them in.

Just as important is putting good things in our bodies. Our marriages work the same way. We always make a priority to include God's Word and prayer in our marriage. We have surrounded ourselves with positive relationships that support our marriage and share like-minded beliefs in regard to marriage. This provides the fuel our marriage runs on. It is vital in creating and keeping a healthy marriage.

Communication (Cardio)

It is suggested that thirty minutes of physical activity every day will help create a healthy body. In a marriage, communication is your cardiovascular exercise. It functions just the same as running or bike riding or aerobics. It is challenging initially, but when we regularly practice it, our endurance builds, and we are able to handle longer distances and longer time intervals. The same suggestion should be made for our marriages. Devote thirty minutes per day to talk (and listen) to each other. This should be done without kids or anyone else, just you and your spouse. A great place to start would be to talk about this book! What have you learned? What is your plan? What are your goals? This should give you plenty of material to talk about!

Over time this intentional time will do wonders and build the health of your marriage. And it will help your marriage with the next part . . .

Trust (Strength Training)

When you speak with a fitness expert, you will learn that strength training is actually the breaking down of our muscles. So, does that mean we should break down our marriage? No, but we should break down barriers so we can be more transparent and vulnerable with our spouse. Our bodies have been created in a wonderful way, such that when we physically break down our muscles, they repair themselves and get stronger. That is the same way trust functions in our marriage.

When we are transparent, when we are mentally and emotionally intimate, barriers are broken down, and trust grows stronger. We have to be careful in this area because if trust is broken, it is just like an injury to our muscles. We can't lift even the weight that used to be easy, and we have to go through a healing process. This

healing process affects the way our body functions. The same goes
for our marriages when trust is broken. Do everything necessary not
to break the trust in your marriage.

Start Today!

Many people begin to address their health after a negative report
from the doctor. I encourage you not to do this in your marriage.
Begin the process today of building and maintaining a healthy marriage. No matter what ring you are wearing or what season your
marriage is in, by addressing the three areas listed above, your marriage can function, thrive, and enjoy optimal health!

Start with You

If after all this you still don't know where to start with your
spouse and your marriage, I've got one last piece of advice. Start
with you.

What do I mean? If you want to work on your marriage, start
by working on yourself. If you want a marriage that is amazing, be
a husband or wife that is amazing! Thankfully, the Bible gives us a
great blueprint for this.

Proverbs 31 Wife

When I say the words, "Proverbs 31 wife," most people, especially married folk, know what I'm talking about. A Proverbs 31 wife
is the true definition of a godly wife. She is a woman her husband
can be proud to call his own, and as the passage says, "She is far more
precious than jewels" and surpasses all women (Prov. 31:10).

For many women familiar with the passage, and those who've
received counsel from women more seasoned in marriage, it becomes
something they desire and strive toward. Here is a snapshot of what
Scripture calls "a capable wife."

1. She rewards her husband with good, not evil, all the days of her life. The Bible speaks harshly against a wife who nags her husband, saying it's better to live on the roof of a house. Instead a wife is to bring good to her husband.
2. She willingly works to produce what is needed for her family. Meeting the needs of her family in this manner excites her.
3. She has sound judgment and makes good decisions, adding value and bringing increase to her family.
4. She is disciplined and strong and fully capable on her own.
5. She is never too busy to help those who are in need. She has a heart for others and doesn't withhold any good.
6. She plans and prepares for her family and helps them present themselves in a way that stands out and is highly respectable.
7. She is resourceful, wise, and a great teacher to her children and friends.
8. She knows what is happening in her household and with her family, and her family knows she is special, and they let her know in the best way they can.
9. She is not only beautiful on the outside, but she loves the Lord and does His will for her life, and this brings honor to her. Although she doesn't need it, she is highly honored and praised for all she does and all she is.

Ephesians 5 Husband

But what about her husband?

Having a true Proverbs 31 wife would be amazing. But it's only half of the equation.

What kind of husband would be the perfect match for the Proverbs 31 wife?

Where is the manual, the blueprint for a man like this?

The perfect man for the Proverbs 31 wife is the Ephesians 5 husband. Like the woman in Proverbs, this brotha has it going on. But I'm guessing, unless you are a serious Bible reader, you may not be as familiar with Ephesians 5 as you are with the passage in Proverbs. Here is a snapshot of the Ephesians 5 husband, the kind of husband God is calling you to be.

1. *Give yourself up for her.* "Husbands, love your wives, just as Christ loved the church and gave Himself for her" (Eph. 5:25). Marriage can be seen as one big journey from selfishness to selflessness. An Ephesians 5 husband will give up *everything* he has in order to make sure his wife has what she needs. No matter how big the sacrifice, meeting her needs becomes his priority.

2. *Keep her clean.* "Make her holy, cleansing her with the washing of water by the word" (Eph. 5:26). My wife was dealing with a troubling situation the other day, and I told her, "I'm willing to be the bad guy." Basically, I was saying: "Put it all on me. I'll get as dirty as I have to in order to keep you clean." Helping her character remain clean is important, and I've found the best way to do this is by learning and living according to the Bible.

3. *Help to reveal her beauty.* "Present the church to Himself in splendor, without spot or wrinkle or anything like that, but holy and blameless" (Eph. 5:27). Our charge is not to dog our wives, or point out her shortcomings but to do all we can to reveal the true beauty we see inside her. We all know the "church" has some issues, but Christ sees something different. Just the same, our wives have some issues, but we are to see and reveal her beauty.

4. *Love her like you love yourself.* "Husbands are to love their wives as their own bodies" (Eph. 5:28). Most people treat themselves better than they treat others. We make exceptions for the same mistakes we condemn in other people. But with our wives, if we are to be Ephesians 5 husbands, we should love and treat her the same way we do ourselves. Ephesians 5 husbands treat their wives with the utmost care and concern.

5. *Get as close to her as possible.* "A man will leave his father and mother and be joined to his wife, and the two will become one flesh" (Eph. 5:31). If you have your Bible out now and are reading along, you'll see the next call to an Ephesians 5 husband is to become one with your wife. The Bible actually says "one flesh." That means to become closer to her than anybody or anything else on this earth. Even if it means separating from other people or things that come against your union. Once you become one, nothing can keep you apart.

Make It About Them

Strive to become the wife or husband the Bible calls you to be, and your marriage can only get better. And one more thing: Ephesians 5 commands wives to submit to their husbands (v. 22) and husbands to love their wives (v. 25). All this boils down to putting more focus on giving value to the other person and less focus on the value you are receiving. That is all. *Make it about them!* I know this is not a groundbreaking discovery, but it is effective when practiced and can change your marriage almost immediately.

Many people enter relationships based more on how the other person (or party) can help them than on how they can help the other person, in both business and personal relationships. Many relationships end when one person feels the other is no longer helping them, when they are no longer receiving the value they expected. The customer is no longer satisfied with the product or service, the employee feels the pay isn't enough or they aren't valued, the employer feels the employee is not producing enough, the spouse feels they are not getting their needs met, or in the case of a writer, like myself, the readers no longer feel the content is valuable to them.

Seldom do you see a relationship end in which one person feels they are the one not providing value to the other person, and they voluntarily choose to end the relationship. Sometimes you may not even realize you are no longer meeting needs or producing enough because you are primarily focused on what you are receiving, not what you are giving. This small perspective change could dramatically change your marriage.

Instead of thinking about what you can receive in your marriage, think about what you have to give. Find out what you can do to serve your spouse, and make that a habit. Many of us can't imagine that, as it's not "normal" to most people. It's not human nature to *not* seek that which provides value to us. I disagree and I believe it is human nature to give value, to create, and to give life to. This in return provides you the value you desire. It seems radical at first, but over time this practice will bring results that would not have been achieved through the "norm." Zig Ziglar says it best, *"You will get all you want in life if you help enough other people get what they want."*[1] If you embrace this one perspective change I believe you will experience radical growth in your marriage, and you will get more in return than you ever have. So let's all change from the "my needs" mind-set to a true "your needs" mind-set, and see what happens.

Conclusion

"Love never gives up, never loses faith, is always hopeful,
and endures through every circumstance."
—the apostle Paul (1 Corinthians 13:7 NLT)

S
o here we are at the end of your journey through *The 7 Rings of Marriage.* I hope you enjoyed the personal stories I've shared from my marriage and those of the other couples we've shared and the lessons we've learned. As you can see, this thing called marriage is made up of many twists and turns. It's made up of many experiences. It's made up of many emotions and many choices.

I would have never imagined in my wildest dreams that one of the most important things I've done to this point in my life was to tell my story and put it in a book for the world to see. But my story, our story, is your story. You're living and experiencing *The 7 Rings of Marriage.* Hopefully this book brings clarity and reveals where you are. And even more so, I hope this book has shown you what is possible for your marriage and the great things you can experience.

You may have already experienced all *7 Rings of Marriage* before you even picked up this book. Maybe you are single and doing your "due diligence" so you can experience all the great things there are to marriage. Either way, if you pull one nugget out of this book that helps you, that is satisfying. If the answer to one prayer is manifested through reading this book, then it is a glorious day. I prayed before I wrote this book. I prayed while writing this book. (Lord knows, I prayed while writing, as it was DIFFICULT!) I'm still praying for you, and I won't stop praying for those who read the book. I would have never written this book if I didn't believe God wanted to use it to bless marriages. I don't know exactly how, and I probably won't be there to see the breakthroughs that happen, but I believe they will because "the prayer of a godly person is powerful. Things happen because of it" (James 5:16 NIRV).

Things are going to happen in your marriage, in your parenting, and in your life. I believe it, and I want you to believe it. I want you to believe for the strongest foundation you could possibly have for your marriage. Then I want you to go out and do the things that will help you create that foundation. I want you to believe for a commitment that knows no limit and a marriage that reaches all the dreams you and your spouse have with each other and for each other. Then dream big and work together to make it all happen.

I want you to believe that there is no end to the things you can discover and learn about each other and living your lives together. Then I want you to become a student of your spouse and spend amazing times together. I want you to believe the conflict you experience in your marriage is like fire refining gold, and what is produced will be more beautiful, more amazing than anything you could have imagined. Then I want you to intentionally work through your challenges together even when it doesn't feel good. I want you to believe that your marriage is not in its final act, that it is like a muscle being broken down only to be bigger and stronger.

Then I want you to do all those things that led you to fall in love and those things that will build up your marriage. I want you to believe that your marriage was created and ordained by God to last and to be fulfilling, and you are living it out right now. Then I want you to enjoy each other in all circumstances, as you never have before. And last, I want you to believe your marriage has a purpose so big that you couldn't see it all because it will extend past your natural boundaries of sight and touch, and the impact will even outlive you. Then teach what you've learned to your kids, other couples; share it on a blog, a book, as a talk, and anywhere God leads you.

I want you to believe all of that for your marriage. And I want you to know I believe it too. I dedicate one day each week to pray for our marriage ministry, those who support us, those who partner with us in prayer and other areas, and you, those who read my writing, watch our videos, listen to our audios, and all the resources Stephana and I share.

We need lasting and fulfilling marriages. Our kids' schools, our communities, our churches, our places of work, our governments— all need lasting and fulfilling marriages. It is the backbone to our society. When marriages break, families break, and it eventually trickles down into every area of society. It is wonderful that God created this union to have so much impact. He created us as relational beings knowing how powerful we can be when we come together. He created us in part to be "fruitful, multiply, . . . and subdue [the earth]" (Gen. 1:28). Embrace it, not just the part that leads to multiplying, and live it. Let the *7 Rings of Marriage* be your guide, your source of hope, inspiration, and encouragement.

I want you to do three things when you put this book down.

1. Pray for and with your spouse that you will have a lasting and fulfilling marriage. Do this immediately.
2. Write down two major actionable items you got from the book, and do them within twenty-four hours.
3. Pray for and share one thing that impacted you from this book with one other couple.

Don't delay on any of these three. This book is about connecting with your spouse, and it's about action. And the big picture is about creating more lasting and fulfilling marriages. We can do this starting with our own marriages and reaching other couples one by one. Maybe one day you'll share your story with me, or how *The 7 Rings of Marriage* impacted your life. No matter what, I'm rooting for you, and I'm praying for you, and I believe your marriage will be everything you hoped and more.

Let me leave you with one thing. Before you were even a thought, before you knew your spouse, before you said, "I do," and before you experienced all that you've experienced in your marriage to this point—God knew. God knew everything that would happen. He knew you'd be reading this book right now. He knew it and He had plans for it. I believe He set the course that led you to come together. Don't let anything stop the plans He has for your marriage and the impact your marriage will have on the world. Your marriage will never be perfect. You will experience major heartaches, pains, and frustrations. But you will also experience inexpressible joy and laughter and peace with your spouse. Cherish it all, as it's part of an amazing plan that is bigger than any one of us and any individual marriage. I'll close with a verse my mother shared with me. This is what Jesus is saying about you and your marriage:

"So they are no longer two, but one flesh. Therefore, what God has joined together, man must not separate."

–Matthew 19:6

Acknowledgments

Wow. How do I even tackle the task of acknowledging all of the people who helped make this happen? My biggest fear is that I'll forget someone, which means this might get lengthy. So, perhaps I'll start with an apology for anyone who may have slipped through the cracks of being acknowledged here.

As with every good thing in my life, there is no way it happens without God. While I knew at some point I'd write a book and share it with the world, when it actually happened, time and time again I felt I wasn't ready. I felt I was not good enough, smart enough, experienced enough, etc. etc.

And time and time again, God confirmed this, in a good way. I was right. I'm not good enough, not smart enough, experienced enough, and not able to complete this task . . . at least not alone. But with Him all things are possible. He is faithful and He will do it. So, I first must acknowledge God's amazing grace, His amazing mercy, and His hand in making this happen from the idea stage all the way to the point where it is in your hands right now.

To my wife, Stephana. *The 7 Rings of Marriage* is you. Without you there is no 7 Rings of Marriage. You've been there from the very first time the idea was put in written form, and you've poured over each and every word since then, to make sure what I've written even made sense. You also held me accountable by making sure what I wrote was being put into practice, at least some of the time (smile). And I can't forget your fervent prayers, your encouraging words, and the sacrifices you made day in and day out. You have been there from day one. Thank you so much. Now let's keep growing closer, keep adding years to our marriage, and keep living our marriage to the fullest!

To my kids, Jaicey, Jackson, and Joshua. You three are amazing! I am so proud to be your dad. You may not have realized how much you sacrificed and how many times you were asked to "let Daddy finish his work." But I realize it and appreciate every minute. You inspired me throughout and helped me push through the tough parts of finishing this book. I loved how you all began writing your own books and stories, or drawing your own picture books (Joshua) when you learned "Daddy is a writer." I hope what I've written makes you proud, and most important, I hope you are proud to be called my children. I love you SO MUCH!

To my mom and dad. Without you there is no me. God chose you two to bring me into the world. You instilled the love of many things in me. Two of the biggest being the love of family and the love of Jesus Christ. Among the many things you've said and done in my life, a couple of them really stand out. Dad, you told me on my wedding day to "be a man for your family." I had no idea what that meant, but it stuck with me and I've done my best to do so. Ma, you shared this quote about your thoughts about grandma, your mom, "A mother's love is the fuel that enables a normal human being to do the impossible. All that I am or hope to be, I owe to my Mother." I couldn't have said it better myself. I love you both!

To my mother-in-law and father-in-law. You have treated me and loved me like I was your own son. Your support, encouragement, and care for our marriage and family is a true gift. Thank you for always being there. Thank you for surprise visits, for giving the perfect gift at the most needed time, and thank you for giving me your amazing daughter to love and spend my life with. I love you both!

To my blog readers, my followers, my subscribers, my web show viewers, my workshop attendees, and my online communities. Without you my voice would not be heard. Without you the words I write wouldn't be shared. Without your feedback, your questions, your critiques, and your encouragement I'd be so stuck! Thank you for reading, watching, listening, and walking this journey with me. I hope you will be forever encouraged, forever find value, and forever be changed by this book and all that I create. Thank you and bless you!

To my mentor, coach, and friend, Dr. Clarence Shuler. When we met a few years back I had no idea how you would impact my life. What I did know was you were a former basketball player, loved tennis, loved Christ, and your wife. So, you were all right with me. But God decided to connect us two former point guards, to help one another and to team up to help marriages. Your counsel, your prayers, your understanding of me, and your example of how to love your wife has helped me in a major way. And not just in completing this book, but in life. Thank you and blessings to you and Brenda.

To Michael Hyatt and Meghan Hyatt Miller, as well as the entire Platform University and Intentional Leadership team. Talk about a "big break." I had already learned so much from you being my virtual mentor, Michael. Without the lessons I learned from your mentorship, my blog and platform might have been dead long ago. And then you invited me to learn from you in person, and to work together on making over my platform. Wow! As they say, "the rest is history!" Thank you and bless you!

To Dr. Thom Rainer. The mentorship, guidance, and advice you gave me, a brand new author, provided comfort and confidence throughout this process. You offered your help, and I had so many questions. Each time you graciously answered them and gave me your advice without delay. It has always amazed me the way you've shared your time with me. I truly appreciate that and I appreciate you! And I truly admire your passion for your family. It is so evident, you are a true family man, who exemplifies real family leadership. Thank you and bless you!

To my writing mentor and friend, Erik Deckers. I was not a very good writer when we met and when you began teaching me. I still have plenty of room to grow, but I am certain my writing would not be worthy of publishing if not for what I learned from you. Your friendship has been just as valuable. And your e-introductions—your e-introductions have resulted in some of the best connections I've made since launching my career as a writer. Thank you and bless you!

To our good friends and prayer partners Mark, Dawn, LaKenya, Alycia, CJ, and Anika. Thank you for your prayers. Thank you for being there. And thank you for proofing, reviewing, suggesting edits, and sharing your thoughts on the book. You all know us very well, and probably walked with us or witnessed many of the stories shared in this book. Thank you for your friendship and bless you all!

To my mastermind groups, my friends, Kevin, Donnie, Eric, Devin, Bryan, Roger, Philip, and Frank. What can I say? Our early morning meetings were amazing. You helped me solve problems, you encouraged me, celebrated with me, questioned me, challenged me, and spurred my creativity. Through it all, not only did I improve my business and writing, but I grew as a person, as a husband, and a father. Thank you and bless you guys!

To my acquisitions editor, Devin Maddox. Time and time again you talked me down from the edge as I had all my first time author questions, doubts, jitters, panic moments, and issues. You encouraged me to "stay the course," and ensured that I didn't need to change every single detail at the eleventh hour, and sometimes the thirteenth hour! I'm thankful you accepted this challenge of working with a first-time author. Your work, your diligence, and your experience helped to make all this happen. And any level of success it achieves does not happen without your involvement. Thank you and bless you!

To the best editor possible for this book, Jana Spooner. I was blessed to not only have you edit this book, but *The 7 Rings of Marriage Bible Study* as well. The way you were able to connect the dots, fill in words I left out, and put it all together in a way that stayed true to my voice, you'd think we'd worked together before, but nope, you are just that good. Thank you for going the extra step with your research, and for immersing yourself into the book. Thank you for not being afraid to say this doesn't work, or this should be changed, or "I took this section out." Any credit is not complete without mentioning you. Thank you and bless you!

To everyone at LifeWay Christian Resources and B&H Publishing Group who played a part in completing this book, the Bible study, sharing the 7 Rings of Marriage, or just took the time to meet me. Your work for the kingdom is immeasurable. Thank you for pouring your hearts and your lives into sharing the truth of God's Word. Selma Wilson, Brad Waggoner, Bill Craig, Amy Jordan, Jennifer Lyell, Jonathan Howe, Michelle Hicks, Amy Lowe, Angela Reed, Rick Simms, Dave Schroeder, Paige Greene, Kim Stanford, Faith Whatley, Tammy Slayton, Linda Denton, Mickey McCloud, Larissa Roach, William Sumney, David Bennett, Nancy Cornwell, Debbie Dickerson, Karen Bell, and the entire LifeWay and B&H family. Thank you and bless you all!

To each of you who helped me along the journey of developing, growing, tweaking, and fine-tuning my platform and brand. Apryl Napier, your fabulous photography has filled my blog with amazing images of me and my family, and the creative photo you took of our hands and wedding rings was the perfect pic for *The 7 Rings of Marriage* book cover. Brandon Triola, your design for my brand, my site, and my eBook was amazing and brought my brand to life. Andrew Buckman, what you did with the customizations for my site took it to a completely new level. Thank you and bless you all!

To the guests for our very first season of the 7 Rings of Marriage Web Show. Mark and Susan Merrill, Kevin and Cetelia Bullard, Clarence and Brenda Shuler, Tony and Alisa DiLorenzo, Dustin and Bethany Reichmann, Lamar and Ronnie Tyler, Justin and Trisha Davis, Talaat and Tai McNeely, Aaron and Jennifer Smith, Jamal and Natasha Miller, and Mike and Kristen Berry, you all shared your marriage and your journey through the 7 Rings of Marriage toward a lasting and fulfilling marriage. Your stories influenced this book and I thank you for our transparency. Thank you and bless you all!

To my church families, pastors, and friends who've prayed, listened, encouraged, and played some role in my life and my family's life during this season. New Horizons Church, Cumberland Road Christian Church, College Park Church, Castleview Church, Heartland Church, Committed for Life Marriage Ministry, Pastor Eric Wiggins, Hank and Denise Mosley, and our Fishers and Greenwood Classical Conversations Communities. Thank you and bless you, your ministries, and your families!

And last, but certainly not least, thank you, for picking up this book and reading it. I prayed for you throughout the process of writing this book. You reading it is literally an answered prayer. It means so much to me that you've taken the time to read any portion of my book. I'm grateful. I thank you and hope that you are richly blessed.

Notes

Chapter One

1. Robert Kiyosaki, *Rich Dad Poor Dad: What the Rich Teach Their Kids about Money That the Poor and Middle Class Do Not!* (Scottsdale, AZ: Plata Publishing, 2011).

2. "Why Marriage Matters," accessed April 29, 2015, http://www.national marriageweekusa.org/images/research/NMW30Conclusions.pdf.

3. Seth Adam Smith, "Marriage Isn't for You," accessed March 12, 2015, http://sethadamsmith.com/2013/11/02/marriage-isnt-for-you.

Chapter Two

1. Stephen Covey, *The 7 Habits of Highly Effective People* (New York: Simon & Schuster, 2013).

2. Kevin Bullard, *Roles in Marriage: Discovering God's Design for a Marriage that Works*, e-book, 2013.

3. "'iysh," Bible Study Tools, accessed March 14, 2015, http://www.bible studytools.com/lexicons/hebrew/nas/iysh.html.

Chapter Five

1. Kevin Bullard, *The 7 Rings of Marriage Web Show,* Episode 003.

Chapter Six

1. Mark Merrill, *The 7 Rings of Marriage Web Show,* Episode 002.

Chapter Seven

1. Natalie Lauren Sims, Torrance Anton Esmond, Charles Dunlap, Le Crae Devaughn Moore, Latasha Williams, Jenny Ingrid Viktoria Norlin, "Buttons." Le Crae, © 2012 by Reach Records.

2. See "fault line," Oxford Dictionaries, accessed March 18, 2015, http://www.oxforddictionaries.com/us/definition/american_english/fault-line.

3. See "earthquake," The Free Dictionary by Farlex, accessed March 18, 2015, http://www.thefreedictionary.com/earthquake.

4. "Why Did the Sacrificial System Require a Blood Sacrifice?" accessed March 19, 2015, http://www.gotquestions.org/blood-sacrifice.html.

Chapter Eight

1. Jon Acuff, accessed April 29, 2015, https://twitter.com/jonacuff/status/74431531191500800.

2. "My Mission to Stop Being Late," accessed April 29, 2015, http://www.sportsdadhub.com/stop-being-late.

Chapter Twelve

1. Zig Ziglar, accessed May 25, 2015, http://www.abundance-and-happiness.com/zig-ziglar-quotes.html.

About the Author

Jackie Bledsoe is a professional blogger, author, and speaker, but first and foremost a husband and father who encourages men to better lead and love their families. He's a contributor to All Pro Dad, Disney's Babble.com, The Good Men Project, and *Huffington Post*. His work has also been featured on Yahoo!, USA Football, MichaelHyatt.com, Black and Married with Kids, Coach Up and more.

Jackie and his wife, Stephana, have been friends since they were teenagers, more than half of their lives, and will celebrate 15 years of marriage in June 2016. They are the proud parents of three beautiful children, and together they co-host *The 7 Rings of Marriage*™ *Show*, where they share practical marriage lessons, and interview couples who have lasting and fulfilling marriages.

The Bledsoes reside in Indianapolis and have a heart for marriage forged through God's grace in their own marriage, which has thrived through homelessness (twice!), job loss and financial despair, loneliness, in-law and intimacy issues. Their desire is for God to use their story as one of hope and inspiration to other marriages.

Find more about Jackie on his blog, JackieBledsoe.com, where he offers some amazing resources created to help you have a lasting and fulfilling marriage and meaningful influence on your kids.

You can also get additional free *7 Rings of Marriage* resources at jackiebledsoe.com/7ringsbonuses.

Want to connect with Jackie? Visit his website, JackieBledsoe.com, and find out how to book him for your next event, read his blog, and connect with him on Facebook, Instagram, and Twitter. Jackie loves meeting and connecting with new people, so be sure to stop by and say hello!

Jackie's blog: www.jackiebledsoe.com
Facebook: www.facebook.com/jackiebledsoejr
Instagram: www.instagram.com/jbledsoejr
Twitter: www.twitter.com/jbledsoejr

STAY STARRY EYED ...
long after the honeymoon ends.

If you enjoyed this book, you'll love digging deeper with *The 7 Rings of Marriage Bible Study*. Explore each of the 7 Rings with your small group as you delve into Scripture, draw closer to the Lord, and invest in your marriage. Through 8 sessions and accompanying teaching DVDs from Jackie Bledsoe, you and your spouse will gain fresh perspective, renewed commitment, and practical biblical wisdom for each stage of marriage. You've learned about the 7 Rings, now it's time to apply each of them, creating a plan for a lasting and fulfilling relationship with the most important person in your life.

Bible Study Kit	*005644102*	**$79.99**
Bible Study Book	*005753519*	**$12.99**

Pricing and availability subject to change without notice.

For More Great Content and Your Book Bonuses visit
JackieBledsoe.com/7ringsbonuses

LEAD AND LOVE
THE ONES WHO
MATTER MOST

Jackie Bledsoe

LEAD AND LOVE THE ONES WHO MATTER MOST